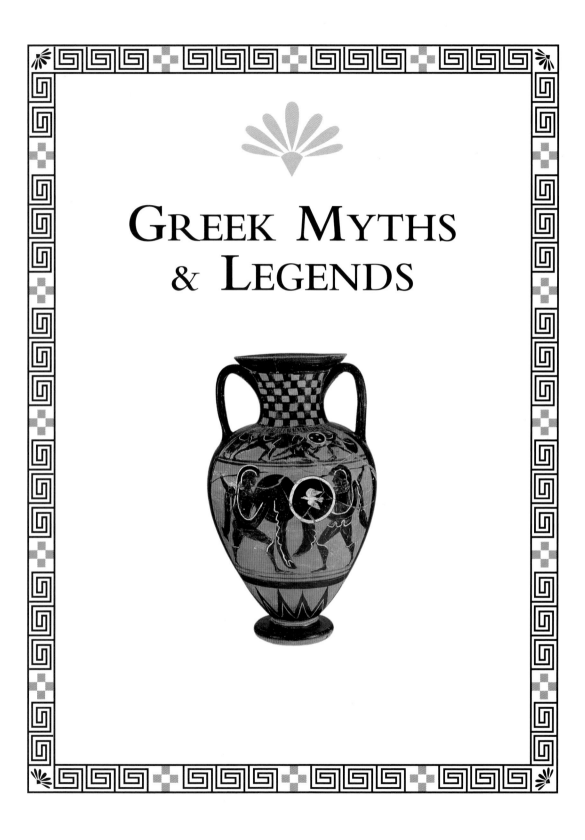

GREEK MYTHS
& LEGENDS

GREEK MYTHS & LEGENDS

DIANA FERGUSON

COLLINS & BROWN

First published in Great Britain in 2000 by
Collins & Brown Limited
London House
Great Eastern Wharf
Parkgate Road
London SW11 4NQ

Distributed in the United States and Canada by Sterling Publishing Co,
387 Park Avenue South, New York, NY 10016, USA

A CIP catalogue record of this book is available from the British Library.

ISBN 1 85585 766 9 (hardback)
ISBN 1 85585 839 8 (paperback)

3 5 7 9 8 6 4 2

Editorial Director: Sarah Hoggett
Project Editor: Katie Hardwicke
Editor: Corinne Asghar
Designer: Claire Graham
Picture Research: Katie Hardwicke
Map Artwork: Alison Lee

Colour reproduction by Hong Kong Graphic and Printing Ltd
Printed by Toppan Printing Co Ltd, Hong Kong

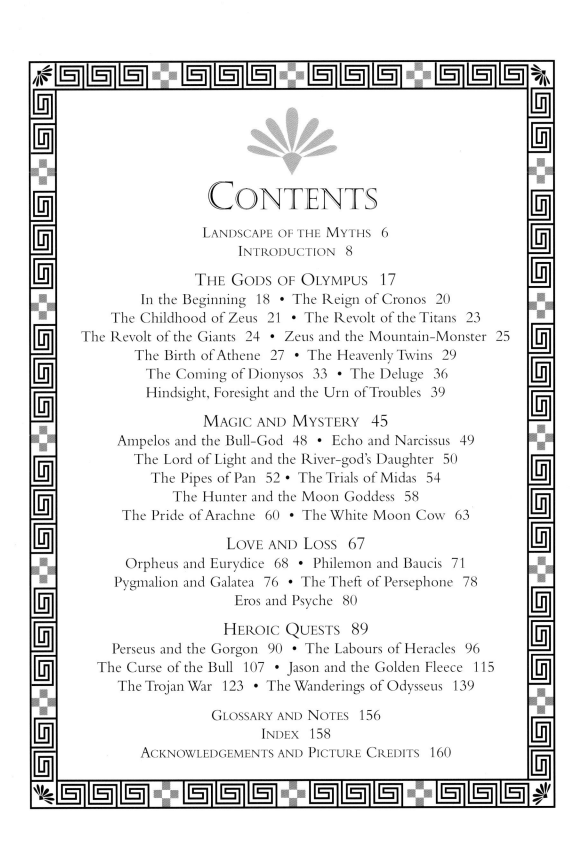

Contents

ITALY

Ionian Sea

THRACE

Aegean Sea

Lemnos

• *Hellespont*

▲Mt Ida

PHRYGIA

Cythera   **Serifos**   **Icaria**

Delos   **LYDIA**

Naxos   • **Ephesus**

• **Knossos**

Crete

Rhodes

Paphos•

Cyprus

Mediterranean Sea

LIBYA

EGYPT

LANDSCAPE OF THE MYTHS

Black Sea

Caucasus
Mountains

COLCHIS

PHOENICIA

▲Mt Olympus

Ithaca

▲Mt Ossa

●Iolcus

ACHAEA THESSALY ▲Mt Pelion

Mt   ●Larissa
Erymanthus▲   Mt Parnassus ▲

●Delphi   BOEOTIA

                    Corinth
Stymphalus●   ●Nemea
Mycenae●   ●Eleusis
Lerna● ●Argos

                                EUBOEA

Sparta●   ●Athens

        ATTICA

INTRODUCTION

VERY YEAR, THOUSANDS OF holidaymakers descend on the Greek mainland and islands – little realizing that they are about to set foot on holy ground. The soil on which they will walk is the same soil once trodden by gods, mythical beings and legendary heroes, for Greece – perhaps more than any other country in the world – has the divine and the magical soaked into the very substance of which it is formed. Water, land, sky, vegetation, even the weather, all have their indwelling spirits. Rivers are not mere water-courses but gods in riverine guise; islands and rocks once had human form; trees and plants were once nymphs. The earth on which people stand is broad-bosomed Gaia, who gives life and takes it back into herself. The dawn that brings the morning is Eos (or Aurora), who streaks the sky pink with her rosy fingers; the sun that lights the day is Helios, who voyages across the heavens in a golden boat; the moon is his sister Selene, who rides the night's highway in a chariot pulled by shining steeds. The thunderstorm is the anger of Zeus, the earthquake the rage of Poseidon – and if it were not for the giant Atlas who holds up the vault of heaven, the sky itself would collapse!

Particular sites also have associations with particular deities or semi-mythical figures. Those who visit Athens, for example, will find themselves under the gaze of Athene, the goddess whose watchful grey eyes keep guard over the citadel. In the Peloponnese, they will encounter the god Pan, frisking in the woodlands – or the warlord Agamemnon, leader of the Greek forces against Troy, and his sister-in-law, the ravishing Helen. Crossing Homer's 'wine-dark sea', they will come to the island of Delos, where Apollo and Artemis were born; or to Lesbos, where the head of Orpheus once sang from a cleft in a rock; and as their boat sails over the blue Aegean they may glimpse the phantom of King Aegeus, father of the Minotaur-slayer Theseus, who threw himself from a sea-cliff because he believed his son was dead.

It is not only on the mainland and nearby islands, however, that holidaymakers may encounter Greek gods and heroes, for their activities took in a far wider geographical range. Far away, on the eastern shores of the Black Sea, they may catch sight of the ghost of Jason, in the act of stealing the Golden Fleece; in the Dardanelles they may see fleeting visions of the Greek encampment around Troy, with Achilles still sulking in his tent over the theft of a slave-girl. Further west, on Corfu – formerly known as Scheria – they may hear the echoes of the voice of Odysseus as he recounts his adventures to King Alcinoüs, while on Ithaca the sounds of a far-off battle may reach their ears as Odysseus despatches his rivals. Finally, if they are brave enough to travel to the very ends of the earth, to the edge of the

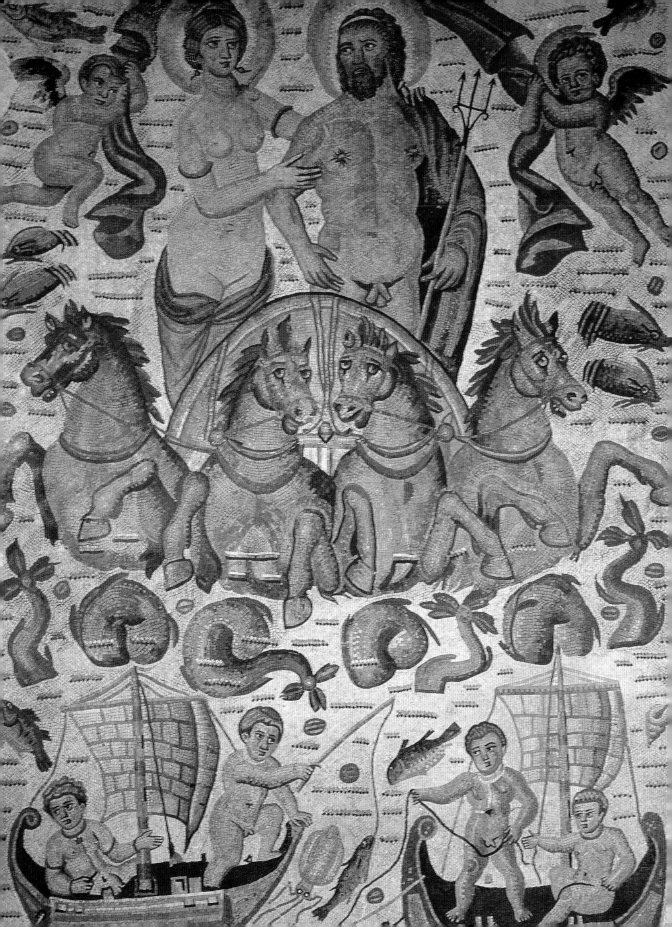

day – the place we now call Gibraltar – they may perceive the spirits of Perseus bearing the head of the Medusa, or Heracles with his stolen booty – the cattle of the sun, and the golden Apples of the Hesperides.

CULTURE AND HISTORY

The widespread presence of Greek gods, goddesses and heroes is not purely geographical, however, for Greek mythology has had an enormous influence on European culture, too.

The most ancient Greek deities, such as Gaia, Ouranos or the Hecatoncheires, were personifications of natural phenomena that helped to explain the world in which people lived. Gradually, other deities were added to this early pantheon, introduced by newcomers to the region or assimilated from other cultures, until finally the large and complex network of gods, goddesses and semi-divine beings that we know today as the Hellenic pantheon was complete. Before the invention of writing, the nature and deeds of these deities would have been recorded orally, in the stories and sagas told by bards; and visually, in the silent language of vase paintings and sculptures. Later, these ancient traditions were drawn on by the poets Homer and Hesiod, and later still by the Greek dramatists.

They were also carried across the water to Italy by Greek expansionists who established colonies and cities there during the eighth century BCE, resulting in a Hellenization of the relatively small Italic pantheon, a process which was complete by the second century BCE. When Rome, traditionally founded in 753 BCE, later established an empire across the ancient world, Roman influence and culture spread, paving the way for the study – by the educated élite, at any rate – of the Classics, the literature of ancient Greece and Rome, and the Greek and Latin languages.

This legacy can still be seen in paintings and literature. In the Italian Renaissance, for example, artists chose one of two main subjects for their sculptures, frescoes and canvases – religious images or scenes from Graeco-Roman myth. The works of William Shakespeare (1564–1616) also make repeated reference to Greek myth and mythical figures; his play *Troilus and Cressida* has as its basis the characters and setting of the Trojan War.

On a more prosaic level, many phrases – 'Achilles' heel'; 'a sop to Cerberus'; 'bearing an olive branch'; 'piling Pelion on Ossa' – have their origins in Greek myth. Once, all educated people, who would have known the Classics, understood such allusions; nowadays, sadly, we need to have them translated for us.

Ironically, it is the Classics themselves that may partly account for the dry-as-dust image of Greek mythology. For many people, learning about the gods and goddesses of ancient Greece conjures up images of worthy and élitist scholarship, and leads them to believe that the myths of ancient Greece cannot be as vibrant as those of other, more 'newly discovered' cultures.

None of this is calculated to fire the imagination or fuel enthusiasm, which is a great pity for once we put aside preconceived notions, Greek mythology turns out to be a treasure trove of beauty, magic and wonder. With the possible exception only of Hindu mythology, the body of myth left behind by the ancient Greeks is probably the largest in the world. The pantheon of gods and mythical beings is absolutely vast. The tales in which they play out their lives are almost endless and cover a geographical range that spans the Caucasus Mountains in the east, north Africa in the south, southern Spain in the west, and Bulgaria in the north.

The meanings of the tales, too, are incredibly rich, for these are stories of gods and goddesses who have evolved over centuries, assimilating the characteristics of other, different deities to produce the multi-layered personae which they present to us today. As with all myths, the sacred stories of the ancient Greeks should never be taken at face value, for there is always a deeper symbolism to be understood. Myths are, essentially, metaphor clothed in narrative: they use the story form to explain the phenomena of the world around them, and encode in their imagery folk memories of events and social changes lost to conscious history.

CRETE AND MYCENAE

The development of the mythology of Greece, and the deities it involves, occurred over many hundreds of years. The mythology as it has come down to us today – with its thunderbolt-wielding overlord Zeus – has its roots in an older and opposing world-view, that of the 'goddess' culture, as exemplified by the religion of ancient Crete. The culture of Crete was a Bronze Age one, but its vision of the world was one inherited from the Neolithic. At its heart was a great mother goddess who manifested herself in all of nature. She was the Great Mother of Life, Death and Rebirth; the Queen of the Sea; the Mistress of the Earth and its Fruits; and the Lady of the Beasts who presided over all animal life.

Because she was 'all of life', the goddess embodied both male and female. Initially, a separate male aspect seems to have been symbolized by male animals – the bull, the stag, the ram – or, even more abstractedly, by the crescent-shaped horns of the bull. Later, representations of a young male god began to appear on Cretan artefacts, but this figure was an infant or at most a youth. His role in relation to the goddess was not that of an equal but of a son. Born of her, he personified the dynamic growth of all life forms that must ultimately die, returning to the goddess who is the source of life for renewal and

11

rebirth. Like the sacrificial kings of ancient times or their surrogate animals, the god had to surrender himself to death in order to engender new life. The god rises, peaks, and falls; the goddess remains, changing but eternal.

When the Mycenaeans – members of a Greek civilization then in its infancy based around Mycenae in the northern Peloponnese – made their first contacts with Crete during the period 1900–1600 BCE, they encountered Cretan culture and came strongly under its influence. As they journeyed back and forth between the island and the mainland, they took this culture with them, adopting it as their own, and finally colonizing Crete itself around 1400 BCE. The Minotaur cycle, which includes one of the most famous of all Greek myths, is of Cretan origin.

The Cretan vision, carried to the Greek mainland by the Mycenaeans, was the finest flower of the old Neolithic Mother Goddess culture which had been widespread throughout the Aegean from the earliest times. As the millennia rolled by, however, other influences began to erode this vision. From 2500 BCE successive waves of Indo-European or Aryan invaders had been entering Greece from the north, bringing with them a totally opposing view of the world. These were peoples whose premier deities were male gods of sky and storm, who saw the forces of nature as hostile, for whom attack and defence were a way of life and the warrior-king was the ideal.

These two systems, one arising out of a settled, agricultural life based around the rhythms of nature, the other the product of a pastoral warrior society, had vied with and accommodated each other until, in 1150 BCE, the Dorians invaded Greece, snuffing out Mycenaean civilization and extinguishing the light of Bronze Age culture in a blaze of Iron Age fury.

A NEW ORDER

The product of these two world-views that had co-existed in Greece was a mythology that allowed for both female and male divinity (although the latter assumed a more dominant position). In the picture language of myth, the gradual shift in the balance of power from female to male is imaged in the form of stories. In the beginning was Gaia, according to the Olympian version of the creation story. Gaia is Mother Earth who brings forth creation all by herself – she is, in other words, a form of the Great Goddess or Universal Mother. Gaia then makes Ouranos, the Sky – who is both her son and her husband – to help her produce a number of offspring including the twelve Titans, the first race of gods. These Titans in their turn create their own progeny; one of them, Rhea, goes on to give birth to the six deities of Olympus: Hestia, Demeter, Hera, Hades, Poseidon and last, the baby of the family – Zeus.

When Zeus leads this younger generation of gods against the older race of Titans and then the Giants, Gaia's patience evaporates and she fashions a monstrous serpent by the name of Typhon and sends him to quell her rebellious grandson. Like the battles between the Babylonian Marduk and the sea-monster Tiamat, and the Biblical Yahweh and the sea-dragon Leviathan, Zeus' contest with Typhon illustrates the victory of a new, patriarchal

sky god over older, primordial forces representing the Great Mother. In his developing family tree, Zeus' position could not be clearer. He is a third-generation god, grandson of the primal Mother and son of the first race of deities, all of whose power he usurps. Furthermore, the site he chooses for his home is a mountain top – Olympus. What better accommodation could an incoming sky god want?

ZEUS, GODDESSES AND NYMPHS

There is one other prickly problem concerning Zeus, however, and that is his endless abductions and seductions of women. Again, if myth is seen as encoded folk memory, these incidents may be read as allegory. When Zeus was first brought by his worshippers to Greece, he saw, everywhere he turned, some manifestation of the old Mother Goddess. As the figurehead of the new patriarchal and hierarchical order, he had to master these female figures. By conquering them, he 'made them his' in a sense and established his overall supremacy; by fathering a whole generation of gods and semi-divine heroes at the same time, he also laid claim, as the new Father God, to the divine power of procreation that had once belonged to the Mother Goddess.

This lust for control in every sphere reached absurd proportions in the myth of the birth of the goddess Athene. Having made Metis, the old goddess of wisdom, pregnant, Zeus contrived to swallow her whole. When Metis was due to give birth, All-father Zeus developed a raging headache and the goddess was delivered – by a kind of cranial Caesarean section – from the head of the god. In translation, what is happening here is twofold. First, by swallowing Wisdom, Zeus is appropriating this attribute to himself; and second, in giving birth from his head, he is elevating the mind as the seat of creative power and denying the body, thereby colluding in the split between spirituality and sexuality that still dogs Western religious thought today.

The continual philanderings of Zeus become almost comic after a time, and are matched only by Hera as the clichéd nagging and suspicious wife. Such stereotypes are superficial, however, and the conflict between this particular husband and wife can be read on a symbolic level as the conflict between the newer, masculine cult of Zeus and the older, feminine cult of Hera – who was, after all, his older sister.

THE THREE-IN-ONE

In Zeus' favour, it must be said that he did at least have the grace to allow a large and continuing feminine presence in his pantheon, unlike other male gods of similar generation in other cultures. As well as the various names under which she manifests herself, the Great Mother may also be detected in the numerous triads with which Greek and most other Indo-European mythologies abound. This threefold multiplicity expresses her very essence. As the divine source of being, she personifies a particular model of the laws of existence; this is not a linear one, in which life ends in eternal death; but a cyclical one, in which death gives birth to new life in an endlessly revolving round.

For ancient peoples, the inspiration for this model was visible on every side. It could be seen in the rhythms of Nature, whereby growth, dying off, and new growth follow each

other in ceaseless cycles. It could be seen in the three recurring phases of the Moon, waxing, full, and waning *ad infinitum,* and in the cycles of human and animal existence.

Such examples provided the basis for the concept of a Triple Goddess, the three-in-one who presided over life, death and regeneration. Following the lunar model, she was Virgin (of birth and the waxing moon); Mother (of life and the full moon); and Crone (of death and the waning moon). Her sacred colours were respectively white, red, and black. The Crone, in particular, might clone herself further, reproducing herself in triplicate to form the ubiquitous threesome of aged sisters with which European myth, legend and story are littered.

One of the most awesome examples of the Triple Goddess in Greek mythology are the Moirae, the three Fates, who spin, measure and cut the thread of life. Less terrifying are the three Hesperides who represent her in her persona as mistress of death and rebirth. Like Eve in her Garden, they tend the apples of immortality, accompanied by Ladon, a serpent of regeneration who has the usual reptilian ability to shed its skin and be 'reborn'.

The single eye and single tooth shared by the three Graeae whom Perseus encounters suggest another tri-faceted unity. The eye and the tooth also symbolize the gifts of perception and divination, while their grey hair suggests old age, both of which link them with Athene in her role as Wise Woman and Crone of Death (wisdom being associated with the enlightenment acquired in the 'otherworld' beyond the grave). Also linked with Athene are the three Gorgons. Their names, 'Wise', 'Strong' and 'Wide-ranging' or 'Universal', allude to the Moon.

Another trinity, the winged Harpies, with their bird bodies and women's heads and breasts, are death spirits. The terrifying Erinyes, or Furies, are a trinity of avenging female spirits associated with the goddess Demeter in her most fearsome aspect.

The famous legend of the Judgement of Paris, in which Paris has to award an apple to the most beautiful of three goddesses, Aphrodite, Hera and Athene, masks another divine female trinity. Far from being contestants in a vulgar beauty competition – as the surface of the tale suggests – the triad are agents of destiny, and it is Aphrodite who gives the Apple of Discord to a reluctant Paris, rather than the other way round, thereby sealing his fate.

All of this is, as it were, what is going on behind the scenes. Although it can enrich our enjoyment of Greek myths, the myths themselves are primarily stories, and it is as stories that they will first be encountered. The tales in this book are no more than a small selection of the wonderful heritage passed down to us. Hopefully, as you read them, these tales of magic and wonder will begin to work their spell on you so that when you have finished, you will find yourself entranced – like the audience of Odysseus who, when that master-teller's tale was done, were left speechless in the listening silence, bound by the skeins of enchantment.

THE GODS
OF OLYMPUS

IN THE BEGINNING

BEFORE THERE WAS EITHER Space or Time, nothing existed but the void of Chaos. In this formlessness, motes and particles and miniscule molecules of matter slowly began to stir. As if drawn by some invisible, primordial force, they gravitated towards each other and clung together in a swelling cluster and a giant shape began to form. When the process of formation was complete, the giant shape rose from out the belly of Chaos like a great whale disgorged by the sea, and floated in the middle of the void.

The shape was Gaia, broad-bosomed, deep-breasted Mother Earth.

Gaia was not alone. Soon after her birth came Eros, Love, the fructifying and vivifying force of creation. Next to emerge from the womb of Chaos was black-winged Nyx, the Night, and her brother Erebos, the dark Underworld. Brother and sister lay together and Nyx brought forth Hemera (Day) and Aether (Space).

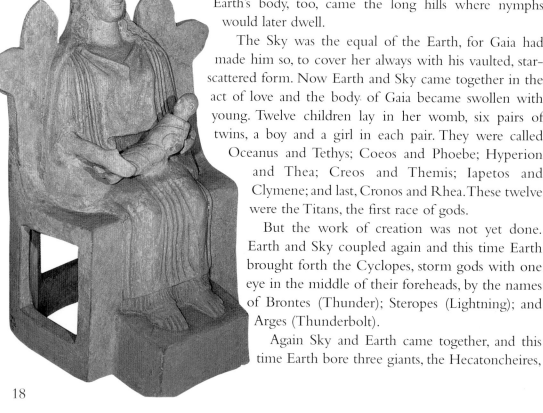

Gaia, meanwhile, was not idle. Unaided, she conceived and bore a son, Ouranos (Heaven or Sky). She also bore Pontus, the barren Sea, so that now Earth was accompanied by Sea and Sky. From Earth's body, too, came the long hills where nymphs would later dwell.

The Sky was the equal of the Earth, for Gaia had made him so, to cover her always with his vaulted, star-scattered form. Now Earth and Sky came together in the act of love and the body of Gaia became swollen with young. Twelve children lay in her womb, six pairs of twins, a boy and a girl in each pair. They were called Oceanus and Tethys; Coeos and Phoebe; Hyperion and Thea; Creos and Themis; Iapetos and Clymene; and last, Cronos and Rhea. These twelve were the Titans, the first race of gods.

But the work of creation was not yet done. Earth and Sky coupled again and this time Earth brought forth the Cyclopes, storm gods with one eye in the middle of their foreheads, by the names of Brontes (Thunder); Steropes (Lightning); and Arges (Thunderbolt).

Again Sky and Earth came together, and this time Earth bore three giants, the Hecatoncheires, who were terrible to behold, for they possessed fifty heads and one hundred arms, and were called Cottus the Furious, Briareos the Vigorous, and Gyges the Large-limbed.

These, then, were the children of Gaia and Ouranos – Earth and Sky – and they wished for nothing more than to roam the world spreading tumult and noise. But the Sky, their father, hated his troublesome brood and decided to banish them from his light and his sight by imprisoning them deep within the belly of their mother. Suffering Gaia, her belly stretched to bursting with so many young, groaned and strained with the burden. She conceived a plan to revenge herself on Ouranos. So she created iron, inside her body, and made from it a great, jagged, many-toothed sickle. Then she called on her Titan sons to avenge her on their father.

It was her youngest who responded, Cronos, Master of Time. When, as was his wont, Father Sky, accompanied by Night, came to lie with Mother Earth, to spread his body over hers and to cover her completely so that no chink of light or space was visible between them, Cronos hid and waited, the great iron sickle in his left hand. When the moment was right, he struck, lashing out with his blade and slicing off his father's genitals in one broad sweep.

Cronos cast the bleeding genitals into the sea, but some of the blood seeped into the body of Mother Earth, and from the drops sprang new offspring, frightful and awesome to behold. There were the Meliae, nymphs of the ash-trees from which warriors would spring in the warlike Third Age of Man. There were the Gigantes, monstrous giants with bushy beards and legs fashioned from huge serpents. And worst of all there were the Erinyes, winged, snake-haired spirits who would, ever after, avenge crimes against Nature, and whose names were Tisiphone the Retaliator, Megæra the Grudge-bearer, and Alecto the Implacable. So terrifying were these Erinyes that mortals would later flatter them with lies, calling them the Eumenides, the Benign Ones, in fear of angering them.

But vengeful spirits were not the only beings to come from the mutilation of Ouranos. As his genitals fell on the sea, a white foam broke out on the crests of the waves and out of this foam a goddess was born. Beautiful, sensual and inflaming desire in the hearts of all who would see her, she came dancing across the waves in an upturned scallop shell, finally settling on the island now known as Cyprus.

The dancing-one's name was Aphrodite.

And so, with the triumph of Cronos the son over Ouranos the father, a new order arose. Sickle-wielding Cronos was also Father Time, and with the beginning of his reign came the beginning of Time.

THE REIGN OF CRONOS

Cronos took to wife his sister Rhea, and together they produced the first high gods of Olympus, daughters by the names of Hestia, Demeter and Hera, and sons by the names of Hades, Poseidon and Zeus. But more of them later, for in the meantime, creation was continuing apace elsewhere to fill the world with a new race of divinities.

Ever-fertile Night continued her task of bearing offspring. Among her many children were Somnus (Sleep); Nemesis (Divine Retribution); Thanatos (Death); and the Hesperides, nymphs who lived on a paradise island beyond the sunset where they guarded the tree that bore the golden apples of eternal life, belonging to Rhea's daughter Hera.

Gaia, meanwhile, brought forth the fateful Moirae, the three spinning sisters who together controlled the thread of life: Clotho the Spinner, Lachesis the Measurer, and Atropos the Cutter.

Every moment, the busy universe seemed to become even busier with the appearance of new gods, goddesses, spirits and otherworldly beings, each of whom immediately laid claim to their personal phenomenon, power or region. It was not long before the world was teeming with their countless divine presences. There was incandescent Iris, goddess of the rainbow. There was Helios the Sun, Selene the Moon, and rosy-fingered Eos the Dawn, all born to Hyperion and Theia. Watery Oceanus and Tethys were delivered of no less than three thousand sons and three thousand daughters, who were all the rivers and water nymphs of the world.

But the work of creation is beyond the understanding of man, and there were aberrations, too, such as the three crone sisters, the grey Graeae, who were born old with nothing but one eye and one tooth to share between them, and who lived in the sea mists of the northern dusk. Their names were Enyo the Warlike, Pemphredo the Wasp, and Deino the Terror.

In the far west, three Gorgon sisters appeared, sisters themselves to the Graeae and equally terrible for they had serpent locks instead of hair and their glance could turn mortals to stone. Just the mention of their names would strike terror into the hearts of men: they were Medusa the Wise, Stheino the Strong, and Eurydale the Universal.

But let us leave the universe to itself awhile and return to Father Time and the birth of his offspring. As each newborn cry signalled the arrival of another child, Cronos shuddered in fear for he had heard it prophesied that he would be supplanted by one of his own blood, just as he had supplanted his own father. He could not let that happen. He devised the simplest of solutions. As each baby was delivered of Rhea, he snatched it and swallowed it whole. Hestia, Hades, Demeter, Poseidon and Hera had already disappeared down Father Time's wide gullet, and Rhea was now pregnant with her sixth child. She was in despair.

'What am I to do?' she wept. 'Am I to lose all my children in this way?'

There was another concern, too. If there was no one to continue the bloodline of the lord of Time, Time itself would come to an end.

Rhea appealed for help to her mother Gaia and her father Ouranos, and wise Mother Earth told her exactly what to do. She must bear the child in secret, and give his father some other object to eat in his stead.

'And when the child is born, I will see to his care,' Gaia said.

And so, on the advice of her mother, Rhea went to thickly wooded Mount Aegeum on Crete – or, some say, Mount Lycaeum in Arcadia – and there, in a dark cave, she brought forth the son who would one day rule the universe. She called him Zeus and gave him into the safekeeping of Gaia. Then she chose a large stone, just about the size and shape of a newborn baby, swaddled it in baby's clothing to conceal it, and gave it to Cronos who, unsuspecting, swallowed it down in one gulp.

Thus the deceit was complete, and Rhea and Gaia saved Zeus from death.

THE CHILDHOOD OF ZEUS

Meanwhile, Rhea washed her newborn son in the waters of a river, and then gave him into the safekeeping of Mother Earth. Gaia took her grandson to Mount Dicte – some say Mount Ida – in Crete, where she, in turn, gave the infant into the safekeeping of two ash-nymphs, Adrasteia and Io, daughters of the Cretan king Melisseus, named after the bee. The daughters of the bee-king fed the divine child with honey, and to drink he had the milk of the goat-nymph Amaltheia. In adulthood, Zeus would not forget Amaltheia and would place her, in gratitude, among the stars, as the constellation Capricorn. To the bee-king's daughters he would give one of her horns, and it would become the Cornucopia, the Horn of Plenty, which was always filled to the brim with whatever food or drink its owner desired.

Even in this mountain paradise, however, Zeus' safety could not be assured and precautions were taken to conceal his presence from his father. So that Cronos would not hear him, the warrior Curetes performed their war-like dances around where the child lay, beating their bronze shields with

their swords to drown out the infant's crying. So that Cronos might not find him in any sphere of the universe, Zeus was placed in a golden cradle which was suspended from a tree, so that he lay neither on earth nor in heaven nor sea.

This, then, was how the child who would be Master of Heaven spent his youth, in a land flowing with milk and honey.

Zeus grew up into a handsome young man, but he knew he could not live for ever in his rural idyll, for he had important business to do. As soon as he reached a certain age, he went to the Titaness Metis, and acquired an emetic potion that would make any who drank it regurgitate what they had swallowed. He then went to his mother Rhea and asked to be made cupbearer to his father. This was easily done, and Cronos, believing he had despatched his youngest son in the same way as his siblings, never guessed the true identity of the new cupbearer who appeared before him, bearing a golden goblet on a golden tray.

'Allow me to present your evening drink, your greatness,' said the wily Zeus. 'I trust you will find it to your liking.'

With one bravura toss of his Titanic head, Cronos downed the entire contents of the goblet in one gulp.

'Ahh. That's better,' he said, and let out a satisfied belch.

And then the emetic began to work.

Cronos was all at once seized by a terrible retching. His stomach went into spasm, he writhed, he lurched, he bent double, he vomited … First out was the stone that he had swallowed instead of Zeus. Another great retch convulsed his body. Out came Hestia. Now Hades. Now Demeter. Now Poseidon. And finally Hera.

As Cronos sank, exhausted, to the ground, all of Zeus' lost brothers and sisters stood before him, surprisingly unscathed considering the length of time they had languished in the commodious chambers of the Titan's stomach. Overjoyed at their release, they hailed Zeus as their saviour.

'You have freed us,' they cried. 'Now you must avenge us against our father and his like – you must be our leader.'

Zeus saw his destiny, spread out before him like a great map. If he conquered the Titans, he could establish a new dynasty. They would set up home in a high place from which he, Zeus, could survey the world. He knew exactly where, too. From the plains between Thessaly and Macedonia there rose a mountain range which on its south face descended precipitously to the Aegean Sea. In the midst of this range was one peak, higher than all the rest. Soaring up to heaven in a single sweep, it hid its head in the clouds. It was Mount Olympus. This would be Zeus' headquarters. From here he would rule the world.

When pressed again to lead the new gods against the old, Zeus, without a second's hesitation, said yes.

THE REVOLT OF THE TITANS

Perceiving the new power of Zeus, the Titans were rallying for war. As their leader they chose the mighty Atlas, son of the Titan Iapetos. Zeus, likewise, was making ready. He descended to deep Tartarus, where the one-eyed Cyclopes and the hundred-handed Hecatoncheires were still held prisoner. He set them free and made them his allies. In return, the Cyclopes gave to Zeus their powers over thunder and lightning. To his brother Hades, they gave a helmet of darkness. To his brother Poseidon, they gave a trident. Under the invisibility granted by the helmet, Hades stole into the presence of Cronos and confiscated his weapons. With his trident Poseidon threatened him, and with his thunderbolt Zeus struck him down.

Then the battle began in earnest. From their fastness on Mount Othrys the Titans launched their attack on Mount Olympus, where the camp of Zeus was based. Zeus answered their assault by showering them with thunder and lightning, while the Hecatoncheires used their hundred hands to pelt the Titans with a rain of boulders. Mountain answered mountain in an uproar that shook the world, that set forests alight, that made the ocean boil, the earth shudder and the sky crack. For ten whole years, the apocalypse continued, as cosmic war raged between the old generation of gods and the new.

At last the Titans were defeated. Zeus sent them in chains to the end of the world, to Tartarus, which lies as far below the earth as the earth lies below the sky. Here, amidst dense shadows and loathsome vapours, they languish to this day.

There were some, however, who escaped punishment. The Titanesses were spared on account of Metis who had helped Zeus, and because of Rhea, his own mother. Atlas, too, was spared imprisonment in Tartarus but received a very special punishment for his part in the battle. He was made to stand for all eternity at the end of the world, bearing on his shoulders the vault of the heavens.

As for the stone that Cronos had long ago swallowed believing it to be his son, this was Zeus' trophy, and he placed it in Delphi at the foot of Mount Parnassus, where for centuries mortals would come to worship and anoint it with oil and make offerings upon it.

But still Zeus could not rest easy on his bank of clouds, for there was more conflict to come before he could assume full mastery of the world.

THE REVOLT OF THE GIANTS

The next adversaries who rose against Zeus were the Gigantes, the snake-legged giants who had been born from the blood of the castrated Ouranos. Angered at the banishment of their brothers, the Titans, they plotted a revolt against the Master of Heaven. Twenty-four in number and prodigiously strong, they emerged from the belly of Mother Earth at Phlegra in the peninsula of Pallene, and headed for Olympus. Their leader was Alcyoneus, and with him were Pallas and Enceladus, Ephialtes and Clytius, Pelorus, Mimas, Polybutes, and others.

As the giants marched, the ground shook beneath their feet. They allowed nothing to stand in their way; even mountains were no obstacle for they simply uprooted them, pulling them up like weeds from the soil. One tore up Mount Rhodope, another plucked Mount Oeta and tossed it into the air, while yet another toyed with Mount Pangaea, balancing the entire mountain in the palm of his hand. Even the dizzying height of Olympus was no deterrent. To scale the citadel of the gods, the giants lifted Mount Pelion and piled it on top of Mount Ossa to build a rocky road to Heaven.

Up on Olympus, the gods were greatly afraid. By now, new deities had been born to swell the numbers of the original Olympians. Some were the children of Zeus himself. There was Athene, and the twins Artemis and Apollo. There was Hermes, quicksilver-swift emissary of the gods, and Dionysos. There was Hecate, queen of the dead, Hephaestus, smith to the gods, the warlord Ares and the goat-god Pan, who would set up home in Arcadia.

But even with this increased population, the Olympians knew that they could not vanquish the giants alone. They knew this because it had been prophesied that the only one who could help them was a mortal, a hero famed for his superhuman strength, a man who wore a lion skin. That man was Heracles.

With Heracles now on their side, the gods felt more assured of victory and the battle began in earnest. The hero began by attacking Alcyoneus, leader of the giants. As Heracles' arrow pierced his flesh, the giant fell down as if dead, but immediately sprang up again, fully refreshed.

'Quick,' called Athene, who was watching, 'Bear him to foreign soil!'

The fact was that Alcyoneus was invincible on the soil of his native Phlegra; it was as if the land itself nourished and sustained him, and restored his life and vigour even when he was fatally wounded.

Summoning every vestige of his superhuman strength, Heracles lifted the giant and flung him beyond the boundaries of Pallene, where he was quickly able to despatch his enemy with his club.

Meanwhile, up on Olympus, mayhem reigned. Porphyrion was pursuing Hera, for whom he had developed a passion after being wounded by an arrow from the bow of Eros, god of love. Heracles returned only just in time to fell him with one of his own arrows. At the same time, Ares had been beaten to his knees by Ephialtes, who had in turn been shot in the eye by Apollo. Again it was Heracles who dealt the final blow, as it was in every case where a god had managed to wound a giant.

The battle raged on but at last the gods claimed victory over the giants. As her trophy, Athene removed the skin from Pallas and made from it her famous *aegis*, her shield or shield cover, so that from that day on she was known as Pallas Athene.

When another of the giants, Enceladus, tried to escape, Athene again acted, hurling a great disc after him as he swam westward across the sea. The missile fell on him, burying him beneath its bulk, and became the island of Sicily. Enceladus still lies beneath Sicily, and when he turns in his sleep the whole island shakes. Nearby lies his brother Polybutes, buried beneath the small island of Nisyros which was hurled at him by the sea-god Poseidon.

And so the giants were vanquished, but still Zeus could not rest easy on his bank of clouds, for there was one last struggle to come before he could assume full mastery of the world.

ZEUS AND THE MOUNTAIN-MONSTER

For decades now, the universe had been in turmoil and there was no peace to be had in any place. Mother Earth, pulled this way and that by the violence of the conflict and angered by the deaths and imprisonment of her children, the Titans and the Gigantes, turned against her grandson Zeus, whom she had once contrived to save. After lying with Tartarus, lord of the infernal regions, she brought forth a monster to send against Zeus, the like of which has never been seen before or since. In the place of legs, he had columns of coiling serpents. In the place of hands, he had serpents' heads. In the place of a head, he had that of an ass. He was so tall he touched the sky, his arms reached a hundred leagues on either side, and he had wings so vast that they blotted out the sun. Fire spurted from his eyes and burning rocks flew from his mouth. He was a flame-spitting, venom-spewing, sky-darkening, walking mountain of a monster.

His name was Typhon and his destination was Olympus.

At the sight of him, all the gods fled to Egypt, where in their terror they did what gods instinctively do in extremis – they turned themselves into animals, Zeus becoming a ram, Apollo a crow, Dionysos a goat, Ares a boar, Hera a cow, Artemis a cat, Aphrodite a fish, Hermes an ibis. Only Athene did not succumb to this ancient instinct and retained her divine form.

Taunting Zeus for his cowardice, she at last shamed him into resuming his normal appearance and taking up the monster's challenge. Zeus began by throwing a thunderbolt at Typhon and flailing at him with a sweep of the iron sickle with which Ouranos had been castrated. Then, high on Mount Casius that looks down over Syria, god and monster engaged in combat, but the god soon found himself entangled in the serpent coils of the monster's legs. Seizing the sickle, Typhon severed the tendons of Zeus' arms and legs, and dragged him into his lair, the Corycian Cave in far Cicilia, north of Aphrodite's Cyprian home. Being immortal, Zeus could not die of his injuries, but they left him completely disabled, and he might be lying in the monster's cave still had not Hermes and his fellow god Pan managed to rescue him from his prison.

With the tendons replaced in his arms and legs, Zeus renewed his attack from the fast-ness of Olympus, hurling thunderbolts at Typhon, who responded in like fashion, hurling mountains at Zeus.

In the battle that followed, the monster fled to Sicily and there Zeus finally felled him by throwing a mountain on top of him. That mountain is volcanic Mount Etna under

which the monster still lies buried, stirring only now and then to spew smoke and fire, lava and ashes out through the mountain's ancient mouth.

And so, with the incarceration of Typhon, the primaeval forces that had so long troubled the world were laid to rest. The tumult ceased, the tempest was stilled, harmony prevailed where disorder had held sway, a new sun shone on a new day, and up in Olympus the eternal reign of Zeus, Master of Heaven and Lord of the Universe, began.

THE BIRTH OF ATHENE

In the boundless long-ago, when the universe was still young and the Earth was just recovering from the after-shocks of her birth, then, in those far-off days, *metis*, Wisdom, first appeared in the world. Metis was the daughter of the Titans Tethys and Oceanus. She was also cousin to Zeus, who had just made himself Master of Heaven. Indeed, Zeus may not have achieved this position had it not been for the help of Wisdom, who gave her cousin the emetic potion with which he overcame his father.

Now that Zeus had achieved his position of supremacy, he looked on Wisdom anew and decided that there was one more thing he wanted from her: he wanted Wisdom herself, to possess her and claim her as his own. At last, after some initial resistance on her part, the god achieved his desire and lay with the goddess, who soon found herself pregnant.

When Zeus heard the news, he went to ask the oracular advice of his grandmother, Mother Earth. Fortunately, it was prophesied, the child in the belly of Wisdom was a girl, and so no threat to Zeus' patrilineal claim to supremacy. Unfortunately, it was also prophesied that the next child that Metis would bear, should she conceive by Zeus again, would be a boy and destined to overthrow him.

Zeus was now beset by a storm of anxieties, and nightmares stalked his sleep. Like his father before him, and his father before that, he feared and hated his own unborn son. The fate of Ouranos, castrated by the hand of his son Cronos, and of Cronos, disabled by the hand of his son Zeus, now awaited Zeus himself. The sins of the fathers festered in the womb of future time, awaiting retribution in the form of the son who would rob Zeus of the one thing he wanted more than anything – to sit for all eternity on the throne of the world. Dark imaginings swirled and took shape in the mind of the Master of Heaven, and his dreams brimmed with thoughts of murder.

Thus it was decided. What Cronos had tried to do to him, he would do to his own.

With honeyed cooings and delicious whisperings, Zeus coaxed the unsuspecting Metis to his bed.

'Come my dearest, come lie with me. Let me embrace you, let me kiss you, let me show you the power of my love …' And in this way he lulled the goddess into a state of supine surrender. She closed her eyes and sighed in anticipatory pleasure.

He watched her for a moment or two. He felt a brief flicker of regret at what he was about to do, but he had no other choice. He gently touched his lips to her hair, then he stretched his mouth wide and wider still until it engulfed the whole of her head, and began to suck her in. Shoulders, breasts, arms, belly, buttocks, legs, all were slowly gulped down by the rhythmic squeezing and pushing of his cavernous gullet, like prey swallowed whole by a snake. The last bit to go was one delicate, wriggling, pink toe. And then there was nothing.

The Master of Heaven licked his lips.

'Well,' he thought smugly, 'that takes care of that.'

For nine whole months, the unborn child of the mother continued to grow in the belly of the father. Then one day, towards the end of this time, when he was by the shores of Lake Triton in Libya, Zeus was seized by a raging headache. It was as if his head was about to burst, as if the plates of his skull were being pushed outward by some great force from within. The pressure was unbearable. He howled and stormed with the pain and, in answer, the heavens howled and stormed, too, raising a tempest of such ferocity that it threatened to crack the sky and bring it crashing down.

Hurriedly, Hermes, messenger of the gods, summoned Hephaestos the divine blacksmith to Zeus' aid. The smith came at once, bringing with him his bronze axe. Raising it, he

slammed it down on the swelling skull of the Master of Heaven, splitting it open like the shell of an egg, and as he did so there rose, phoenix-like from the cleft in the cranium, a magnificent figure, fully formed and fully armed and terrible to behold. She was Athene of the shining eyes, goddess of war and, like her mother, goddess of wisdom, and as she rose she let out a shout of power that ricocheted off the faces of heaven, earth and sea and resounded through all the spaces of the universe.

Thus, by swallowing the mother and giving birth to the daughter, the father claimed wisdom and all creative power as his own.

This was Zeus' version of events, but rumours persisted about Athene's true parentage and nature. This daughter of an Olympian had some very un-Olympian traits. How, for example, did she come by her *aegis*, her shield? Was it really made from the skin of the giant Pallas, whom she had destroyed as some said, or did it, as he claimed, belong to Zeus? But *aegis* is a goatskin and *pallas* means 'maiden', which hinted at foreign genes for this so-called child of Zeus. Could it be that this Athene was the Virgin Goddess of the goatskin-wearing girls of Libya, land of her birth, and that she had come to Greece of her own accord by way of Crete? And what of her predilection for snakes – crowning her hair, fringing her garment, writhing on the Gorgon's head that she placed on her shield – hissing serpents that warn away the unitiated and, as they slough their outworn skins to be born anew, embody the power of regeneration? Such things are women's secrets, and it was even whispered that Athene had no father at all, let alone a Greek god, and that she had given birth to herself in an act of spontaneous creation, Wisdom begetting Wisdom.

On all these questions, Zeus of course remained silent.

What is sure is that the citadel and later city that has stood for three thousand years on the plain of Attica, looking out to the blue Aegean, belongs to the divine presence whose name is simply 'Goddess' – *A Thea*. Athens is the city of Athene, and on its hill her shrine still stands: it is the Parthenon, the temple of Athene *Parthenos*, Athene the Virgin. When Poseidon wished to win the city for himself, he offered a spring of gushing water and the horse. But Athene offered the fruitful olive tree, and the city has been hers ever since. For three thousand years, she has guarded and protected it. If the gods and the fates will it, may it be hers for thousands more.

THE HEAVENLY TWINS

Many are the tales told of the lustful urges of Zeus and of the divine children he thereby begat. One such tale concerns a goddess by the name of Leto, daughter of the Titaness Phoebe, the pure Moon, and the Titan Coeus, the Ball of Heaven.

Leto's abode was said to be in Asia Minor, and some say that she was Zeus' wife before Hera. When the pair coupled they did not do so as god and goddess, but in the form of two quails. After this bird-union Leto found herself pregnant, not with one child but two.

But even amongst the gods matters do not always run smoothly, and Leto was destined to suffer greatly before she would be delivered of the divine twins she was carrying. A curse had been laid upon her that she might not give birth in any place where the sun shone, where there was no more light than in the *lykophos*, the wolf-light that we call dusk, when only wolves can see. Some blamed Hera for this, saying that in her jealousy she had cursed Leto. Furthermore, they claimed, she had sent the serpent Python to harry the pregnant goddess from place to place so that nowhere dared give her sanctuary.

Whatever the truth of the matter, Leto found herself roaming the wide world searching for a haven where she might spend her confinement. Borne aloft on the wings of Notos, the South Wind, she sailed along on the updraughts of air like a bird who has lost its way,

ATHENS AND THE PARTHENON

THE SITE ON which Athens – the city of Athene – stands was first inhabited around 3000 BCE. Later, in the Mycenaean period (*c.* 1600–1200 BCE), it was home to a major palace and fortification, probably the centre of a small kingdom. Mycenae, after which the period takes its name, lay to the south-west of Athens, and had become the centre of power in Greece. The age over which it presided, however, was one preoccupied with war and defence, against both overseas enemies and neighbouring kingdoms (the Trojan War, in which Greek forces were led by the Mycenaean overlord Agamemnon, may recall Mycenaean attempts to expand into Asia Minor and to control Black Sea trade routes).

Given this background, it is not surprising that Athens, as an important Mycenaean centre, should offer special veneration to Athene in her oldest manifestation – that of goddess of war. As Athene *Promachos*, she was the one who 'fights in the foremost ranks'; as Athene *Alalcomeneis*, she was the one who 'repulses the enemy'. The protectress of towns and guardian of citadels, she was the subject of a special cult in Athens.

Appropriately, the temples dedicated to her stood on the Acropolis, or citadel, of the ancient city. As well as the temple of Athene Nike and the Erechtheum, she also had the Parthenon, the temple of Athene *Parthenos*, or Virgin (here 'virgin' does not relate to notions of virtuous chastity, but to the qualities of independence and self-determination). Designed by the architect Ictinus and with sculptures by Phidias, it was built from about 450 BCE during the age of Classical Greece, which was directly descended from Mycenaean civilization.

As well as being a goddess of war, Athene was also, by extension, the deity who controlled the ending of war. The olive branch, taken from the tree which was her gift to Athens, came to be a symbol of peace. A sacred olive tree, dedicated to Athene *Pandrosos*, goddess of the olive, grew in her sanctuary, the Pandroseion on the Acropolis.

seeking refuge in Attica, in Euboea, in Thrace and in all the islands in the blue Aegean from as far south as Crete, but all refused her pleas for entry. At last there was only one place that Leto had not tried: Ortygia, Quail Island, a barren crag barely visible above the waters, whose bulk was hidden in the dark depths of the sea.

Now every story conceals another, and that is as true of this tale of Leto as any other. Leto once had a sister by the name of Asteria who, like her, had been pursued by Zeus and who, also like her, had changed herself into an ortyx, a quail, to escape him. No sooner had she done this, however, than Zeus transformed himself into an eagle and was about to overtake Asteria, when she changed shape again, turning herself into a large stone, and in this guise plummeted to the waters below, where she was at last safe. Here she continued to float, moving at the whim of the waves like seaweed on the swell of the tide. So it was that Ortygia was formed, and it was to this Ortygia that the desperate Leto appealed.

'Help me!' she cried. 'My time draws near, my children are about to be born – do not let us die beneath the sea! Give me shelter and the son I will bear, who will be more glorious than any god ever seen, will build a great temple on your stony soil, and your name will be famed throughout the world and great wealth will be yours.'

Hearing these words, the little island consented and rose from the waves, baring its flanks to the sun where no sun had shone before, and allowing the South Wind to lower Leto gently onto its soil. Now that it was no longer hidden in the depths of the Aegean, it changed its name: it became the island of Delos, the Brilliant, the Visible Star, and the gods anchored it to the sea-bottom with four stout pillars.

Thus it was, on the island once called Ortygia, that Leto bore her first child, a daughter by the name of Artemis who would be the virgin goddess of the moon's light, who would be served by handmaidens called *arktoi* – she-bears – and who would love nothing more than the chase and to hunt the beasts of the forest with a bow made of silver.

Thus it was, on the island now called Delos, that Leto bore her second child, a son by the name of Apollo. But unlike that of his sister, his journey into the world was long and hard and caused his mother much suffering. All the goddesses of Olympus had come to attend her labour, save Hera and Ilithyia, the divine midwife. She was unaware of Leto's need for her because Hera had obscured Delos behind a bank of cloud. The little island, too, awaited the infant's arrival with unsuppressed excitement, exhaling sweet fragrances which perfumed all the air around it, while singing swans wheeled and circled overhead.

Attended by the solicitations of goddesses, the singing of swans, and the wafting of scents, Leto endured the pains of childbirth for nine whole days and nights. At last, unable to bear her suffering any longer, the goddesses despatched

Iris, goddess of the iridescent rainbow, to fetch Ilithyia, promising her a necklet of gold, nine ells long, in reward, and with this gift the one goddess persuaded the other to accompany her to Delos, both disguised as turtle doves.

Down on the island, Leto's travails continued. Bracing herself between a palm tree on the one side and an olive on the other and pressing her legs against the soft soil, she gave one final, mighty push and – just as Ilithyia set foot on Delos – shining Apollo was born and, so the bards recall, the earth beneath him smiled. The goddesses cried out for joy, the swans – who had circled eight times – ceased their circling, and all around was bathed with gold. The leaves on the olive tree turned to gold. The river Inopus flowed gold. The very foundations of the island itself turned to gold. Thus the world welcomed the child who would be the golden god of the sun's light.

The goddesses took the infant and washed him in clear water, and wrapped him in white swaddling clothes bound with a girdle of gold. Then the goddess Themis fed him nectar and ambrosia, which is the food of the gods, and the child burst out of his swaddling bands with all the precociousness of his divinity and spoke, saying:

'The lyre and the bow will be mine, and I will be an oracle of divine truth to humankind,' and at these words Delos burst into blossom.

And later, when Apollo first appeared in Olympus with his lyre in one hand and his bow in the other, all the company rose as one from their seats, and the Muses began to sing. Then nine goddesses – Hebe, Harmonia, Aphrodite and her attendants the three Graces and the three Horae – joined hands in a circle around him and, accompanied by the god's own sister Artemis and the gods Ares and Hermes, all began to dance. In their midst stood shining Apollo – Apollo *Musagetes*, Lord of the Muses, Apollo *Kitharodos*, Singer to the Lyre – plucking on the strings of his instrument as if with a plectrum of sunbeams and, as the bards have it, making music out of sunlight and causing all of Heaven to sing.

THE COMING OF DIONYSOS

If all that is true is no lie, then it must be said that Zeus the All-high, Master of Heaven and shape-shifter extraordinaire, was an incorrigible womanizer. Neither goddess nor woman was safe from his attentions, so keen was he to spread his seed. Not for him the paltry excuses or feeble alibis of philandering human husbands, for Zeus was a god and his seduction strategies dazzled with divine ingenuity.

Of late, looking down from his pinnacle on Olympus, the Great One had been watching the ravishing Semele, daughter of Cadmos, king of Thebes. He decided to pay her a visit. But on this occasion, the guise he adopted for the seduction was uncharacteristically humble. He appeared to Semele as neither a bull, nor a snake, nor a swan, nor a shower of gold, nor as a swirling, shifting mist – as he had, and would, in other places and other times and with other women. No, on this occasion, the mask he chose was the most cunning of all. He appeared as an ordinary mortal man. No glory shone from his face, no brilliance from his eyes, no rumbles of thunder attended his presence, no crackles and flashes of lightning. He looked as human as you and I.

Semele was totally beguiled. Inevitably, one thing led to another and it wasn't long before Zeus found himself where he had intended to be all along – in Semele's bed. Inevitably, one thing led to another and it wasn't long before Semele found herself pregnant by Zeus. Inevitably, one thing led to another and it wasn't long before Hera, wife to Zeus, discovered what had been going on, under her very nose, down in the palace at Thebes.

Well, what a husband can do, a wife can do equally, and Hera – with delicious irony – chose precisely the same strategy as Zeus to make contact with Semele. She changed her shape, adopting the appearance of someone in whom Semele trusted totally – her own nurse. The likeness was so exact that had you been there to see it, you could not have told the difference between the false nurse and the true, even down to the hairs on the old dame's chin. Thus was Semele caught in the web of deceit between husband and wife, thus did the spider-skeins of fate begin to wind themselves invisibly around her.

By now, the god's beloved knew her lover's true identity, but he had consistently appeared to her only in mortal form, a fact which Hera seized upon with gleeful anticipation.

'My dear,' she whispered conspiratorially to Semele, 'a word in your ear if I may … now I know you have a lover – anyone can see that just by looking at you, you're so radiant and glowing - and I know who he is, too. None other that the great Zeus himself! There is one little thing that worries me, though – and you know I speak as one who has your best interests at heart – and that is, why does he never show himself to you as he really is? If he really loved you, he would hide nothing from you. Ask him to prove his love – ask him to show himself to you as he shows himself to Hera!'

Hera, of course, knew precisely what would happen should Zeus accede to this request. And that was precisely what she wanted to happen.

Hera's words began to prey on Semele's mind. Why did Zeus never truly show himself to her? Surely love depended on total honesty and openness? Did he not trust her? The seeds of doubt, so well planted in the fertile soil of her imagination, took root and flourished.

On Zeus' next visit, Semele curled up to him.

'My dearest,' she began, 'if you truly love me, will you grant me one little request?'

Zeus, satiated with lovemaking, was oblivious to all instincts of alarm and was effusive in his reply.

'Name it!' he said, waving an arm expansively in the air. 'Name what you will – your wish is my command!'

'Well,' began Semele tentatively, 'what I would really like, you see, is for you to show yourself to me as you show yourself to Hera.'

How chillingly these words rang in the ears of the Master of Heaven. They brought him back to his senses with a thud. He had, however, given his word, and his word he must keep. Semele watched with growing fascination as before her very eyes her lover began to change. He seemed all at once to grow in stature, as if he would burst the bounds of the room. His skin began to glow, his eyes to shine. Scintillating sparks of light fizzed and popped around him, and tongues of fire licked his skin. With a roll of thunder that shook the palace walls and a flash of lightning that cracked the night sky, Zeus revealed himself to Semele in all his glory. She was no longer looking on a man, but on a god – the greatest god of all. No human could do that and live. And so it was that hapless Semele, object of a god's desire and victim of a goddess's revenge, found herself ignited by her lover's incendiary presence, and consumed in a blaze of divine fire.

But there was still the matter of the child in her womb, a boy, as it so happened. It is said that, as the mother burnt, tendrils of ivy miraculously grew up out of the floor of the chamber and coiled themselves into a living shield to protect the foetus from the flames. Be that as it may, what is known is that Zeus managed to retrieve the unborn infant, and tucked him into his thigh for safekeeping, where he could continue to grow to full term.

When the moment arrived for the child to be born, Zeus went to Mount Nysa where he delivered himself of his son. Dionysos was the baby's name and, because he was twice-born – once from his dying mother's body, once from his father's thigh – he was known as Dionysos *Dithyrambos*.

The divine child was given into the care of the nymphs of the mountain, and thus spent his childhood and youth in the company of women, an upbringing which, it has to be said, resulted in a quality of unmanly softness, an effeminacy.

There was something, too, of the animalistic and primitive in this son of Zeus, for when offended the god would visit swarms of serpents, proliferations of vines and ivy, and madness on those who failed to respect his laws. Reared by women and beloved of women, he would grow to be Dionysos *Mainomenos*, the god of divine mania, and would have a band of female followers called the Maenads who, inspired by him to raging ecstasy, would tear their victims apart with their bare hands, during their rites in the mountains and wild places.

But of all the qualities for which Dionysos is famed, he is known as the god of wine, and it was to spread knowledge of viticulture that the god travelled the world – accompanied by his retinue of satyrs and Maenads, playing flutes, tambourines, and drums and bearing the thyrsus, the god's ivy-twined, pine-cone-tipped staff – passing through Thrace, Boeotia, Attica, Aetolia, Laconia, the Aegean islands, Phrygia, Phoenicia, the Caucasus, Mesopotamia (where he crossed the Tigris on a tiger and the Euphrates on a rope-bridge of ivy tendrils and vine-shoots), India, Libya and Egypt, before returning home to take his place among the Twelve Great Ones of Olympus.

Many, many generations on, we still have Dionysos to thank for the priceless gift of that magical elixir that has within its depths the power to liberate the human soul – for the briefest span – from the chains of the human condition.

THE DELUGE

Far off in his mountaintop eyrie on Olympus, Zeus the All-High, Lord of the Sky and Master of Wind, Cloud and Thunder, was looking down at Earth, and he was not pleased. The problem, in short, was mankind.

Not only had mortals acquired skills in the many arts that properly belonged to the gods, but they had also claimed the better part of the ritual sacrifice which, with fire stolen from heaven, they were now able to cook to succulent readiness, and all with the connivance of the Titan, Prometheus.

In addition to these impertinences, there was the problem of Lycaon. Lycaon was ruler of Arcadia, and it was he who had instituted the worship of Zeus in the kingdom. On one particular occasion, however, he had offended the god by sacrificing to him a real, live boy, one of his own kind, made of human flesh and blood. The odious gift was repugnant to Zeus because it reeked of the ancient cannibalistic practices of the region. To show his displeasure, Zeus had changed Lycaon into a wolf.

However, there were still Lycaon's sons – some had counted twenty-two, others said there were near on fifty – who seemed to have learned nothing from their father's metamorphosis, and were behaving just as reprehensibly as ever. Zeus decided to pay them a personal visit, disguising his true identity by adopting the garb of a humble traveller.

GREEK TRAGEDY

BOTH 'THEATRE' and 'tragedy' are terms of Greek origin. 'Theatre' comes from *theásthai*, to behold. 'Tragedy' is believed to come from *trágos*, goat, and *oidé*, song. The link between 'goat-song' and the drama we know as tragedy is unclear, but it has been suggested that it may be connected with the ritual catharsis of the festivals and mysteries of Dionysos, the sacrificial god.

In Athens, there were three great tragedians, working when Athens was at its cultural peak and all drawing on myth for their subject matter. The first was Aeschylus (525–456 BCE), the 'Father of Tragedy'. Formerly, dramatic presentations had involved a single actor and the chorus; by introducing a second actor and elevating dialogue above the role of the chorus, Aeschylus effectively founded the tragedic form. Only seven of his works remain, including *Prometheus Bound*.

Sophocles (496–406 BCE) eventually overtook Aeschylus in popularity. He increased the number of players to three, and wrote tragedies that were on a less heroic scale, revolving around such semi-mythic characters as Oedipus and Ajax.

Finally, Euripides (480–406 BCE) produced tragedies which showed human beings in a realistic way. He is said to have written 90 plays; those that have survived feature figures such as Heracles, Medea and Odysseus.

The brothers welcomed him and offered him the hospitality of their table, but then had the affrontery to put before their guest a soup made of the entrails of sheep and goats, but also containing the entrails of their own brother, Nyctimus, whom they had murdered.

Zeus was outraged. He leaped to his feet, threw over the table on which his hosts had served the loathsome stew, and changed them all into wolves, just like Lycaon before them.

Back on Olympus, he pondered. All mortals were clearly beyond redemption. There was only one thing for it. He would have to destroy mankind.

So the Thunder-thrower and Master of Heaven sent to earth a Great Rain.

It was barely noticeable at first, falling as a fine mist, but soon the volume increased to a pitter-patter, and then the raindrops became heavier until gradually the fall had become a torrent that hammered down on the rooftops like giant nails thrown by some unseen celestial hand. It rained and it rained and it rained and it didn't stop even when the rivers had swollen to overflowing and burst, carrying whole cities away with them as they surged to the sea. The deluge raged for nine whole days and nine whole nights, submerging everyone and everything.

When, on the tenth day, the rain ceased and the flood was calmed, the whole world had been transformed into a vast, shimmering lake, stretching north, south, east and west. Nothing else was visible except for the highest mountain peaks, piercing the water … and a small wooden ark, bobbing on the surface like a toy boat. Inside it were two humans, Deucalion and Pyrrha.

Once again, the Titan Prometheus, benign trickster and protector of mankind, had interfered in the Thunder-thrower's plans for the human race, for Deucalion was his son, and Pyrrha, Deucalion's wife, was the daughter of Epimetheus, the Titan's brother.

With his gift of foresight, Prometheus had warned his son of the impending deluge, and Deucalion had at once built the wooden vessel, filled it with provisions, and, with his wife, taken refuge while all around them the tempest raged. At last, when the storm had abated, the ark came to rest on Mount Parnassus.

When the waters had subsided and the land again appeared, the pair stepped out into an uninhabited wilderness of devastation. They sacrificed to Zeus, pleading humbly with him, as protector of fugitives, to repeople the earth. Then they picked their way slowly to the ruined shrine of the Titaness Themis, where they again prayed.

In answer, Themis herself appeared to them.

'Veil thy head,' she said, 'and throw the bones of thy mother behind thee …'

The bones of thy mother? What bones? There were no bones here. There was mud a-plenty. There were broken branches and battered trunks uprooted by the force of the torrent and tossed hither and thither; there were rocks and stones, washed clean of soil and plant life; there was flotsam and jetsam of all kinds; but there were no bones.

'… throw the bones of thy mother behind thee.'

Slowly, like the seeping sunrise, realization dawned. The Earth was their mother and her bones were the rocks and stones that lay all about them.

Deucalion and Pyrrha veiled their heads. They each picked up a stone and threw it over their shoulders, and in the place where each missile fell a person stood instead. Those that Deucalion threw became men and those that Pyrrha threw became women.

These men and these women are our ancestors for it is they and their children and their children's children who have multiplied to repeople the world, in all the generations that have come before us, and for all the generations yet to come.

HINDSIGHT, FORESIGHT & THE URN OF TROUBLES

This is a story of warring generations, of feuding and dynastic struggle, of cunning and cruelty and, ultimately, of the destiny of man.

The tale begins with four brothers, the sons of a Titan. The eldest was Atlas, who ruled a vast land that lay in the western ocean, called Atlantis. Then there were Menoetius, Prometheus – 'Foresight', so-called because of his gift to foresee what might come – and last, Epimetheus – 'Hindsight', so-called because of his gift to reflect on what had been.

The relationship between the old race of the Titans and Zeus had never been good. This was understandable since Zeus, himself the grandson of Ouranos and son of the Titan Cronos, only narrowly escaped being eaten at birth by the latter. But there was something in Zeus' nature that was more than righteous filial anger. There was a tyrannical streak, a vindictiveness, a competitive drive for power, that coloured everything he did.

For his part in the Titans' rebellion against the Olympians, Zeus had already punished Menoetius by striking him down with his sky-god's thunderbolt and sending him deep as deep can be, down into infernal Tartarus and eternal damnation.

Atlas was found guilty on two counts. First, or so the Master of Olympus alleged, the Titan had allowed greed and wickedness to flourish in his kingdom of Atlantis (although the kingdom's enviable natural wealth was probably the real crime). Second, like his brother Menoetius, he had dared to rise against the Olympians. The punishment Zeus meted out was two-fold. First, he destroyed Atlantis, allowing the Athenians to overrun it and then submerging it beneath a great flood, where it has lain ever since, for ever lost and for ever sought. Next, he commanded Atlas, whose size and strength were unmatched, to stand for all eternity at the edge of the world, holding up the sky.

That left just Prometheus and Epimetheus.

With the wisdom of his foresight, Prometheus had been clever. Knowing in advance the outcome of the Titans' revolt, he had chosen to fight on the winning side, and had given his allegiance to Zeus, persuading Epimetheus to do the same.

So it was that Prometheus was invited into the charmed circle of Olympus.

Prometheus was the wisest of his race, and had learned many skills from Athene – the arts of healing, the study of the star-patterns of the heavens, how to work in metals, how to plot and piece with numbers and measurements and calculations, and many other wonderful secrets as well. These he had passed on to mankind so that they began to excel at these things, too, much to the annoyance of jealous Zeus.

It so happened one day that all the gods and people of the earth had come together at Sicyon to decide which portion of the ritual sacrifice rightly belonged to the gods and which to men. Prometheus was placed in charge of the division of the sacrificial beast – on this occasion, an enormous ox. Having cut up the animal in his own way, Prometheus began to lay out the portions. On one side, he arranged the succulent flesh, the moist entrails, and all the other tender delicacies that the sacrifice contained, and these he covered with the coarse skin of the beast. On the other side, he placed the carcase and bones, which he disguised under a layer of rich white fat. Then he invited Zeus to choose which portion he considered most fitting as a divine offering. Lured by the succulent covering of fat, the greedy god naturally chose the portion of bones, whereupon Prometheus removed the fat to reveal what lay beneath, shaming Zeus as a gullible fool.

In a fit of spite, Zeus retaliated.

'Let humans have the better portion – but let them eat it raw, for I will deny them fire!'

But clever Prometheus, who had always helped mankind, knew a way around the god's petulant decree. He instantly went to the island of Lemnos, to the forge of Hephaestos, the blacksmith of the gods, where the sacred flame burned, and here he stole a few of the burning embers, secreted them in a fennel stalk, and took the gift of fire to the people of the earth.

Such defiance was a foolhardy thing, but a greater trouble was yet to come.

If Zeus could not deny fire to mankind, he could at least make sure they paid dearly for it. He had a particularly entertaining revenge in mind. He ordered Hephaestos to fashion from clay and water a maiden of irresistible beauty, the first mortal woman. Her skin had the luminosity of porcelain, her langourous doe-eyes were fanned by soft lashes, her lips were full, her hair the colour of beaten copper, her breasts and hips rounded, her wrists and ankles slim, her feet and hands delicate and pink-tipped. Never had such a beauty been seen. The four winds breathed into her the breath of life, and all the goddesses of Olympus adorned her.

Her name was Pandora, and Zeus sent her to the mild Epimetheus to be his wife. But Epimetheus, much to the god's surprise, demurred:

'Too kind … really, I couldn't … no, please, I could never …'

THE AGES OF MAN

IN THE STORY OF Pandora and the release of all the Troubles into a hitherto untroubled world, we are in the presence of one of the grand archetypes of myth, that of a half-remembered Golden Age or Paradise from which mankind has been excluded, and to which we can never return. In this time and/or place there is neither cold nor hunger nor pain nor sickness. The inhabitants do not age, and they might not even die. They live with the gods, and are as gods. In this dream-state, time itself might not even exist.

For the Greeks, this pre-partum paradise belonged to the first phase of existence, known as the Golden Age. This was when the first human beings lived as subjects of Cronos, who was son of Gaia the Earth and Ouranos the Sky, and father of Zeus – it represented a pre-Hellenic and pre-Olympian age. These first people lived in total bliss, free of worry, fatigue and old age. They fed on wild honey and wild fruits, drank the milk of sheep and goats, and spent their days in continual merriment. Although they were not immortal, death descended on them like sweet slumber, after which they became guardian spirits for the living. Historically, this image alludes to a pre-agricultural era when the bee-goddess was worshipped.

Next was the Silver Age, peopled by a race of farmers who ate bread – feeble men who, ignominiously, 'obeyed their mothers'. The allusion to farming and the eating of bread shows that agriculture (the growing of grain)

had been introduced, while obedience to mothers suggests a matriarchal age. Silver, the metal of the female Moon, has similar matriarchal connotations. Such an opposing system would have been presented unfavourably by a later, more patriarchal age.

Traditionally, the 'mother's boys' of the Silver Age were destroyed by Zeus, who ushered in the ensuing Bronze Age. In this, warriors dropped from the ash-trees, armed with bronze weapons. They were hard-hearted and delighted in war and slaughter, and ate flesh as well as bread. A second and more noble race of warriors followed, who were born of gods and mortal women, and became great heroes. Historically, the first race alludes to the earliest Hellenic (Greek) invaders of the region, who were Bronze Age herdsmen and would have brought with them beliefs about a typically Indo-European sky god such as Zeus. The second race suggests the warrior-kings of Mycenaean Greece, an ancient civilization which flourished c.1600–1100 BCE. It glorified the warrior ethos, typified by such heroes as Achilles of the Trojan War.

The final age was that of Iron, peopled by the worthless descendants of the Bronze Age warriors. Nothing good can be said of them, for they lacked honour, respect, courage and any desirable virtue. From a Mycenaean point of view, this perfectly describes the Dorians, the last wave of Hellenic invaders who swept down from the north and conquered the Mycenaeans with their iron weapons.

And he returned his bride-to-be to Zeus. This was not an easy thing to do for he was a man like any other, but he had been forewarned. His brother Prometheus, in his greater wisdom, had told Epimetheus on no account to accept any gifts from Zeus, for no good would come of them.

Such a refusal was a foolhardy thing, but a greater trouble was yet to come.

Zeus was speechless with rage to discover that once more Prometheus had blocked his plans. The act of vengeance he now settled on was perhaps the most vindictive and cruel the Master of Olympus had ever committed.

He devised for Prometheus a torture of more exquisite refinement than has ever bedevilled the imagination of gods or men. He had the Titan stripped of all his clothes, lashed to the crest of Mount Caucasus, and sent an eagle to devour his liver.

All day, the eagle gorged itself, pecking away at the blood-rich organ and tearing out chunks of oozing flesh. All night, the liver grew whole again for it, like Prometheus, was immortal. That, Zeus knew, was the real beauty of his invention.

The next day, the eagle would come again to eat, and that night the liver would faithfully regenerate itself once more to provide the next day's feast. And so on and on it was destined to continue for thirty years or thirty thousand years, all to appease the Master of Olympus, release from the torture only coming when the hero Heracles at last set Prometheus free.

Such a cruelty was the unkindest thing, but a greater trouble was yet to come.

When Epimetheus saw his brother punished in this gruesome way, he decided, with the benefit of hindsight, that it might be wiser to do what Zeus wanted.

'Perhaps I was a little hasty … now that I have had time to think it over … well, yes, I could do with a wife …'

And the luscious Pandora was returned to him, and the marriage celebrated forthwith, as Zeus had wished all along.

This is when the real trouble began.

Now there was in the house where Prometheus had formerly lived with his brother, and where Epimetheus now lived with his wife, an urn. The object was, in truth, something of a mystery. How it got there is not entirely clear. Some say it was a wedding gift from Zeus that Pandora brought with her, others that it was there before, under the guardianship of the good Prometheus, now languishing in chains on a faraway mountaintop.

Whatever the urn's origins, Epimetheus and Pandora had instructions not to open it, a prohibition which, as Zeus knew all too well, the inquisitive Pandora would find hard to resist. Every day, whenever she saw it, tucked away in the corner of the room, she wondered. What could it possibly contain that should not be discovered? Gold and jewels beyond the dreams of avarice? The elixir of youth? The secret of eternal life? (Both of these were of particular interest to her because, unlike her husband, she was not immortal.) Magic powers that would confound the gods? Some sprite who, imprisoned in the urn for a thousand years, would grant all her wishes in gratitude for his freedom?

Her imagination ran wild, and the hidden contents of the urn became an obsession – Pandora just had to see for herself.

So she waited until Epimetheus was out and she would not be disturbed. She crept quietly over to the object of her fascination. The urn was large and heavy, about waist-high, and fashioned of coarse terracotta with a rough terracotta lid. On the lid was an inviting handle, of the same material.

Pandora placed her hand on the handle, and began to slide the lid away. Its earthenware base scraped against the earthenware lip of the urn. She moved the lid some more, until just a chink of the interior was visible.

Suddenly, without warning, there was a blast from within the urn and the lid blew off. Pandora was thrown backwards as a swirling whirlwind of chattering, jibbering demons spewed forth in ebullient release. First out were Sickness and Old Age and Sorrow, then Madness, Greed and Evil; Hatred fluttered its wings in the throng, accompanied by its sibling, Jealousy. There, too, were Infirmity, Blindness, Poverty and Toil, Guilt and Shame. The demons that emerged from the urn were so numerous that they all but blotted out the light.

Now Pandora understood. The beings that she had so unwittingly released from bondage were the many Spites that wished to afflict humanity, and that had, up to now, been imprisoned in the urn.

The Spites stung Pandora in every part of her body, then darted off – a black, buzzing, droning swarm – to sting mankind and implant their poison deep in their blood for ever.

But the urn was not quite empty. A small, bedraggled, bird-like creature was the last to emerge. It shook its wings, perched momentarily on the lip, looked around, then flew off after its companions.

The small, bird-like creature was Hope.

And so it was, and so it is, that with the coming of all the afflictions that have plagued mankind ever since Pandora first opened the urn, Hope came too.

And so it was, and so it is, that through all the dark thickets and mazy ways of life, where illusion and disappointment bait their traps and hardship and sorrow lurk, there too is Hope, the bright white bird in the forest, that makes bearable the bonds of the human condition and saves the Soul from Despair.

MAGIC AND
MYSTERY

AMPELOS AND THE BULL-GOD

LONG AGO AND FAR AWAY, in a golden land warmed by the sun, where the days were cloudless and blue and the black-velvet nights sparkled with the glitter of a million stars, there lived a youth called Ampelos. Ampelos had liquid honey eyes and sun-gold skin and long, supple limbs, and he was more beautiful to behold than any other boy or man.

One day, when Ampelos was slumbering unawares on the bank of a river, a rowdy troupe of travellers came by. With cymbals a-clashing, flutes a-warbling and bells a-jangling, these were the noisy followers of Dionysos the bull-god, Dionysos son of Zeus. When the god came upon the golden youth, fast asleep, he silenced his rabble to a hush and gazed on Ampelos. Seeing that he was fairer than anyone he had ever known, he loved him as a lover does his beloved.

Dionysos stayed in the place where Ampelos lived, and the god taught the youth many new things. Ampelos was his favourite, and he became ever more like him, in dress and manner.

But one day, Dionysos became troubled by dark dreams concerning the fate of his dear one – dreams that foretold that Ampelos would be gored to death on the horns of a bull.

Under the tutelage of the god, the youth had learned to hunt and feared none of the wild beasts that roamed the land. But now, Dionysos warned him, he need fear no animal save one – the wild bull, the very animal that was sacred to the god himself.

Time passed and in the passing of time, Ampelos had all but forgotten the god's warning when one day he happened to be wandering alone in an isolated spot and there, in a clearing ahead of him, he saw a bull. It was a magnificent beast. Its body was stout and broad, its legs strong and agile, its head proud, its horns sharp, its eye keen.

Stealthily, Ampelos crept closer. The bull watched him, making no attempt to move but for the soft shush-shush of one hoof on the ground. The youth came even closer. He reached out and stroked the animal's back. The bull still seemed docile and a bold idea entered Ampelos' head: he would go for a bareback ride. The bull offered no resistance and, using the horns as leverage, the youth mounted the animal's back, and they were off.

They hadn't gone far, however, when a gadfly, sent perhaps by the goddess Selene, began to buzz around the bull's head. Irritated by its small tormentor, the bull changed its trot to a canter and its canter to a gallop, almost unseating its rider in its attempt to escape. Foolish Ampelos, to be deceived by the beauty of a bull! As the animal jumped to avoid a rock in its path, the rider was thrown forward over its head, like a helpless rag-doll, and impaled on its long, sharp horns. The horns sank deep into his soft flesh, piercing his breast, and then, moistened by the flow of wet blood, let his body drop. Limp and fatally wounded, Ampelos lay on the ground and slowly bled to death, feeding the thirsty earth with his rich, red blood.

The beloved of the bull-god had been gored to death by a bull.

When Dionysos discovered Ampelos, he was overcome with sorrow. He dug a grave and tenderly buried his body in the earth, as a farmer plants a seed in the soil.

Summer passed and winter came, bringing a covering of snow over the grave. Then spring arrived and soft rain watered the spot where Ampelos lay buried, and a tiny green shoot broke the soil. The shoot grew and twirled and twined its way upward like a column of smoke reaching for heaven, and broad leaves grew from its branches and then dense clusters of small, round, juicy fruits.

Dionysos came and picked the fruits and crushed them in his hand and tasted the juice and it was sweeter and more potent than anything he had ever tasted before. The fruit was the grape and the juice was wine. Thus, from the body and blood of Ampelos, a new elixir had come. And Dionysos gave the elixir to mankind – the magical, mystical potion that slays the demons that infest the soul, that warms the heart, that opens the way to enlightenment, that leads us on the path to heavenly joy.

ECHO AND NARCISSUS

Once, when the world was young, when the mossy-green velvet of the forest swathed hill and valley, when the air was clear as glass and dawn brought days of kingfisher blue, when spirits inhabited every tree and rock and river and stone, there lived a mountain nymph called Echo.

In most respects, Echo was like her sister nymphs. She danced on the grass like them, she bathed in the mountain pools like them, she made garlands of meadow flowers like them – but wherever she was, whatever she was doing, she had one problem: she could not keep her mouth shut. In short, Echo was an incurable chatterer.

Ordinarily, this small affliction would have been no more than an irritant to those around her. But when, like the great goddess Hera, you are trying to keep track of your philandering husband and his flirtations, such ceaseless prattling distracts you from your task. Every time, just as Hera was about to pounce on Zeus' latest favourite, along would come the garrulous Echo …

'Good morning, Hera, what a beautiful day, is it not? No, wait, please don't hurry by … more haste, less speed, I always say … but what a cross frown that is … now you know that frowning gives you wrinkles … just remember, a smile a day keeps the wrinkles away … and don't forget – with a happy song you can't go wrong …'

And so on and on as Echo launched into one of her long-winded stories, allowing Hera's rival to make good her giggling escape.

Well, Hera had finally had enough. She turned to Echo:

'Day after day you have detained me with your endless tittle-tattle. Well, from now on, you will be silent. The only time you will open your mouth is to repeat the words of others!'

'…words of others!' said a somewhat startled Echo.

Doomed never again to have any speech of her own, Echo retired from the company of others and sought solitary refuge among the gorges and glens of the mountains.

And that was where, one day, she first laid eyes on Narcissus.

He had come to the mountains to hunt, and Echo had never seen anyone so handsome before. Like many before her, male and female both, she fell in love with him on the spot. Her passion was misplaced, however, for Narcissus' own heart was as cold and unreceptive as rock, and he was totally incapable of feeling love for another.

Of course, Echo knew none of this, and secretly followed Narcissus through the glen, wondering how – with no words of her own – she could ever speak her love. As she flitted unseen behind him she inadvertently stepped on a twig on the forest floor which snapped with a crack, alerting Narcissus to her presence.

'Who's there?' he called.

'… there?' replied Echo.

'Come out, show yourself! I won't hurt you.'

'… hurt you.'

Driven by her desire for him, Echo at last emerged from hiding and approached Narcissus as if to embrace him, but he pushed her away roughly.

'Don't touch me!' he cried.

'… touch me!' echoed Echo sadly, as she watched Narcissus vanish into the trees.

Up in Olympus, Artemis, goddess of the chase, had been watching, too. She remembered the hunter's many rejected lovers; she especially remembered Ameinius, who had killed himself for love of Narcissus and who had asked the gods to avenge his death. She decided to teach Narcissus a lesson: he would, after all, fall in love, but with someone who was as unobtainable for him as he had been for others.

Unaware that he was being watched, Narcissus had continued to run through the forest until at last, exhausted, he stopped to rest by a quiet pool. The glassy surface of the water was as still and smooth as a mirror, and as he bent over it, he saw his own image. What a beautiful face! It was the most handsome face he had ever seen and he immediately fell madly in love with it. He reached out to touch the apparition in the water but, as his fingers broke the surface, the image shattered in the spreading ripples.

He tried once more, but it was useless. Every time he reached for his reflection it fragmented at his touch. And so he languished by the poolside, lovesick and tormented until, unable to endure his suffering any longer, he took a dagger and plunged it into his own heart and, bleeding, died. The earth drank up his blood and when it was satiated, it gave forth a small and delicate lily-like flower, with a heart the colour of flame and petals the colour of new cream.

That flower was the narcissus, and it may still be found today, growing wild in dappled forests and by woodland streams and pools.

As for Echo, the sorrow of unrequited love was too great for her to bear and she slowly pined away, her physical form vanishing to nothingness until all that remained of her was a sound – the sound of her voice, which may still be heard to this day, echoing among all the lonely crags and crannies of the world like the mournful call of a ghost.

THE LORD OF LIGHT AND THE RIVER-GOD'S DAUGHTER

Fair of face and comely of body, the lord Apollo radiated the sun's light wherever he went. Good looks were not his only asset, for he was a master musician, drawing from the strings of his lyre airs of such poignant sweetness that they brought tears to the eyes of all who heard them.

Now you would think that, with such charms at his disposal, Apollo would have been irrestible to women, but this was not always so, and in some cases his pursuits ended in misfortune for those with whom he was enamoured.

One such case was that of Daphne, a nymph who was the daughter of Peneios, god of the river of the same name that flowed through Thessaly, and priestess of Gaia, Mother Earth. Apollo had first seen Daphne and her fellow nymphs bathing in the region's limpid pools – as nymphs are wont to do – and had been fired with desire for her, for her beautiful face, her smooth skin, the feminine curves of her body. But before he was able to declare himself to her, someone pre-empted his plan – Leucippos, the 'white stallion'.

This Leucippos had also conceived a passion for Daphne, but where Apollo's approach would have been direct, his rival chose more underhand methods. In order to infiltrate the company of nymphs and get closer to the object of his desire, Leucippos had dressed himself as a maiden and thus, by the simple strategem of donning women's clothing, had found himself easily accepted into their society. With mounting irritation and jealousy, Apollo watched from on high as Leucippos frolicked girlishly with his companions, giggled as they played games, coyly allowed the others to dress his hair, altered the timbre of his voice to join in with their lilting singing, and feigned fainting fits so that the nymphs, deceived by this play-acting, would minister to him, taking his head in their laps to caress and fuss over him.

But Apollo, being a god, was more than equal to the ploys of any rival in love. He put it into the nymphs' heads that they should take their new friend to their favourite pool and there – to cool themselves from the heat of the day – divest themselves of their clothes and bathe naked.

The nymphs thought this an excellent idea and could not understand the reluctance of their new companion to join them in the water.

'Come on in!' they called. But as Leucippos still hovered on the edge, apparently too shy to reveal his nakedness, the nymphs playfully pushed him in and, with numerous tickling fingers, removed his clothes.

Well, what a sight met their eyes! Where were the maidenly breasts like theirs? Where the roundness of hips and thighs? The soft downiness of skin? There were no such traits to be seen here; the physiognomy of this particular nymph was altogether different from that of the rest.

The nymphs, who only moments before had been tender, soft and gentle, now showed their other face. They became wild, angry and raging, and to show Leucippos their fury at his deception, they fell upon him and, with their bare hands, tore him limb from limb.

With Leucippos out of the way, it was now Apollo's turn.

The god waited a few days for calmness to descend once more on Thessaly, and then he made himself – and his feelings – known to Daphne.

'I wish to love no man, neither god or mortal,' replied Daphne in response to his overtures.

Undeterred, and with unshakeable conviction in his powers of attraction, Apollo merely took this refusal as a sign of maidenly shyness. He persisted a little harder, for his ardour demanded satisfaction.

But still Daphne resisted. Apollo was astounded. It had never occurred to him that he – Lord of Light, Master of the Lyre, seer and poet – would be turned down by any woman. Like his father Zeus before him, he just could not take no for an answer.

'Well,' he thought, 'such reticence will merely add spice to the chase,' and he put his arm around Daphne's shoulders and attempted to kiss her. The nymph brushed him away, but the more she resisted, the more determined he became. She managed to break away from him and began to run down towards the river Peneios.

'Help me!' she cried out, 'Help!', as she felt the thundering footsteps of the god coming ever closer.

It was Gaia who heard her cries and just as Apollo was closing in on her – just as he was about to wrap his arms about her – Daphne disappeared, and where she had stood only seconds before, there now stood a laurel tree. Thus Apollo, lord of light, found his lusts thwarted. Thus, instead of holding a girl in his arms, he found himself standing, rather sheepishly, with his arms tightly clasped around a tree.

Ever since then, the laurel has been sacred to Apollo, and he has worn a crown of its leaves on his head. And because he is the god of poetry, the 'laureate' – a laurel wreath – is the honour conferred on all who excel in this art.

THE LAUREL

In the ancient world, poetry and prophecy were closely connected; poets were seers, gifted with all-knowing, and capable of uttering great and mystical truths. In Classical Greece, both poetry and prophecy were linked, through the god Apollo, with the laurel. According to myth, Apollo, god of poetry, claimed it as his own when the nymph Daphne metamorphosed into a laurel tree in order to escape him.

Apollo's gift of prophecy was acquired by blatantly dishonest means. Having first tricked the Arcadian god Pan to reveal the secret art of prophecy, Apollo then went on to lay claim to the Delphic Oracle, where enquirers might obtain information about the future. The Pythoness, the priestess of the Delphic Oracle, was now in Apollo's service and wore a crown of laurel leaves.

Laurel wreaths were conferred on poets, and awarded to the victor at the Pythian games, held every four years at Pytho in Phocis, on the southern edge of the Greek mainland. Pytho later became Delphi.

Because of the ancient belief that the laurel embodied the spirit of poetry and prophecy, a custom grew up of placing the leaves under one's pillow to absorb their potency as one slept, thereby achieving poetic inspiration and the power of foresight.

THE PIPES OF PAN

Imagine an idyllic land, where fat flocks graze in green pastures, where shepherds and shepherdesses while away the drowsy hours weaving daisy-chains from meadow flowers, where honey-rich hives hang heavy in the woods, where the wolf does not strike, where hunger does not lurk, where sadness is not seen. Imagine Arcadia, long, long ago.

It was in this Arcadia that an ancient god had made his home. Half-man and half-goat – in beard, horn, tail, and leg – he was the Lord of the Wildwood, the Horned God, the mischievous, frisking, lustful, lascivious, fiendish, devilish Pan.

Pan presided over Arcadia. It was Pan who guarded the sheep and cattle, who made the ewes fertile, who tended the bees, who brought the hunters their game. It was Pan whose unseen presence, in the strange noises in the mountains or in the sudden rustling of the leaves, could cause a wave of *pan-ic* in the breast of the unwary traveller. When the mountain nymphs enjoyed their nightly revels, it was Pan who would be at their midst, shiny horns a-glinting and cloven hooves a-prancing, looking for all the world like Satan himself dancing by light of the moon.

Pan loved all the nymphs, but not in a brotherly way. In fact, none was safe from his promiscuous attentions. Some, like the chaste Pitys who ended her life as a fir-tree, escaped him, but others succumbed to his doubtful charms. His greatest conquest was achieved with guile when he seduced Selene the Moon, concealing his goatish hairiness under a fluffy white fleece.

One day, while roaming Mount Lycæum, Pan's eye fell on the nymph Syrinx, daughter of the river-god Ladon. What a delightful sight she was, with her exquisite face and voluptuous figure! He would have to get to know her. A little idle chit-chat would do to open the proceedings.

He boldly stepped out from among the trees, and began.

'Where are you going, my pretty, my dear?' he cooed, slipping into the well-worn patter known to every sweet-talking seducer.

'Down to the river,' the nymph replied.

'Who waits for you there, my sweetheart, my love?'

'My sisters are waiting for me.'

'What will you do there, my lovely, my fair?'

'I'll have a swim in the water.'

'How long till you get there, my honey, my sweet?'

'Very soon, if you detain me no longer.'

'Detain you?' cried Pan, snapping out of his sinuous chatter, 'What makes you think I want to detain you? No, indeed, I'll not detain you, I will come with you, to see you safely to your destination. After all, a girl can't be too careful … there are some strange people in these parts …'

And Pan slid into step beside Syrinx. But, of course, patience was never one of Pan's virtues, and in no time at all, he had sidled closer to the nymph, so close that their bodies almost touched and her nostrils were filled with his pungent animal smell. She could feel his hot breath on her neck. He reeked of sexual menace. She felt very uneasy.

Before she knew what was happening, Pan had lunged at Syrinx and tried to catch her in his embrace, but she broke free and ran, calling out her father's name, towards the river.

Pan stayed close on her heels but just as he thought he had gained his quarry, just as he was about to wrap his arms around her, he found his arms wrapped around – an armful of reeds!

The river-god had changed his daughter into a reed, indistinguishable from all the others.

There was only one action that Pan could take. If he could not have Syrinx herself, he would have the next best thing. So he bent down and cut a bunch of reeds, trimmed them to size so that each was slightly shorter than the last, fastened them together in a neat row, and fashioned for himself a new kind of pipe. He called it the Syrinx, after the nymph that got away, but others call it the Pan-pipes.

Pan did not pine long for Syrinx for, just as there are many fish in the sea, so there are many nymphs in the wood. He always kept his pipe with him, though, and often played it to amuse himself – and who knows, perhaps its sweet airs went some way to compensate for his coarse appearance and were an aid to him in his determined pursuit of love.

THE TRIALS OF MIDAS

Here follows the tale of the unfortunate Midas, king in Thrace and later Phrygia, who liked to speak without thinking first and who landed himself in a great deal of trouble.

THE GOLDEN TOUCH

It was always known that Midas would one day be rich. When he was but a babe in his cradle, a stream of ants was seen carrying grains of corn and placing them between his sleeping lips. Such a portent, the soothsayers foretold, meant only one thing: the baby was destined for fabulous wealth.

When grown to manhood, Midas planted a famous rose garden around his palace, and into this perfumed plot one day rolled an elderly and rather effeminate figure, Silenos by name. Silenos was the tutor of the goatish Dionysos, wild god of wine and divine intoxication. On this occasion, the aged reveller had partaken too joyously of the god's ecstatic draught, and had broken away from the crowd to sleep it off in Midas's garden, among the scents of musk and honey.

This was where the king's gardeners found him, with petals for his pillow and roses in his hair, and immediately brought him before their master.

Midas welcomed Silenos and found him, now sober, a most amusing guest. Silenos proved to be an accomplished weaver of tales, and entertained king and company with a gossamer web of fables and fancies which told of a vast continent beyond the ocean with magnificent cities in which giants dwelt, and of trees with magical fruit that could reverse the process of ageing, so that whoever ate them became younger and younger until finally they reached the moment of their own conception, and vanished into the nothingness beyond.

These were the marvels of which Silenos spoke, and with which he entertained the court for five full days and nights. At last, however, Midas realized that the old tutor should rejoin his divine pupil, and sent him, accompanied by servants, after Dionysos.

The god was grateful for the return of Silenos and for the hospitality he had received, and to show his gratitude told Midas that he would grant him whatever wish he wanted.

'You have only to name it …' was the god's message, '… name your heart's desire.'

What treacherous words these were for mortal ears. With the voices of the soothsayers of his youth echoing in his mind, Midas did not hesitate. He had only one heart's desire: gold.

'I wish that everything I touch shall be turned to gold,' he said.

No sooner said than done: the king's wish was granted.

To try out his new skill, Midas reached down and tapped the sandals on his feet. In an instant, what had once been strips of leather was now a fretwork of gold! He touched one of the palace walls. It, too, turned to gold! He went into the garden, where his beloved roses grew. He fingered the thornless stems. Gold! He stroked the leaves. Gold! He caressed one of the blooms. Gold! His hand brushed a bee feeding on one of the flowers. It, too, instantly mutated into a hard, golden pellet and plummeted to the ground.

He was a wizard, a magician, and soon he would be the richest king in all the world! Like a madman possessed, Midas tore around his palace, swooping on everything he could lay his hands on and transmuting it to gold with his alchemist's touch.

As dusk fell, Midas – exhausted but jubilant – waited for his servants to bring him his usual meal, consisting of the sorts of delicacies that would tempt jaded royal palates. His triumphs of the day had whetted his appetite, and he selected a particularly choice morsel of meat, redolent with spices and meltingly tender as butter – but no sooner had he touched it than he felt it harden under his fingertips. It was a lump of solid gold, and totally inedible. He let it fall, with a clatter, onto its plate.

He next reached out for a fat, purple fig, its skin splitting to reveal the ripe, pink flesh within. But as his hand closed on it, it became a gilded replica of itself, perfect in every detail but as useless in sustaining the body as dry dust.

And so it went with everything Midas tried to eat – even the wine in his cup was changed to a molten gold soup at the first sip.

That night, for the first time in his life, Midas went to his bed hungry.

From now on, no matter how hard or ingeniously he tried to circumvent his alchemical powers – ordering his servants to feed him, pecking at food speared on a stick, sucking up wine through a hollow reed – it was useless. Without nourishment, Midas began to waste away. Hollows sucked in his once-chubby cheeks, and his round, royal belly shrank.

At last he realized that what a man wants is not always what he needs, so he went to the god Dionysos and asked him to remove the gift he had been given, which was really not a gift after all.

'Go to the mountains, to the source of the river Pactolus,' said the god. 'Bathe yourself in the fountainhead, and you will find yourself cleansed.'

And as Midas immersed himself in the cool, limpid waters of the spring, he saw a golden dust wash from his skin and float away on the current. His golden touch was gone … but it did not disappear altogether for traces of it may still be found in the alluvial gold of the Pactolus river.

THE ASS'S EARS

If Midas had been a wiser man, he would have learned from this experience … but he cannot have been a wise man for his foolish tongue was once more to land him in trouble.

It all began easily enough, with a musical contest beween two brothers, known as Babys and Marsyas, and the god Apollo. At first, Marsyas had had no instrument on which to play and was forced to remain silent while Babys trilled out simple tunes on his single-piped flute.

But one day all this changed. While idling along the riverside, Marsyas happened upon something that looked like the bone of a deer. On picking it up, he realized that it was not one, but two hollow bones, sculpted and smoothed and fastened together to form a double-piped flute – the first of its kind that Marsyas had ever seen. What he did not know was that the flute had been fashioned for her own amusement by none other than the great goddess Athene herself. On catching her reflection in the water as she played it, however, and seeing how comical she looked, the goddess had discarded it … and now it belonged to Marsyas.

Marsyas put the flute to his lips and blew – and, oh, what a sound came out! It was the song of the skylark, the music of the spheres, the harmonies of heaven all rolled into one – and *he* was playing it! He practised some more, and as he did so, his confidence grew. Jigs and reels, airs and laments, medleys and variations, caprices and études, all floated effortlessly from his pipes – and all delivered with such talent, such bravura, such panache! Why had he never realized his own genius before now? It was time to reveal this colossus to the world.

Marsyas decided to take on the greatest challenge a musician can – he decided to pit his skills against those of Apollo *Musagates*, Master of the Lyre and Lord of the Muses who inspire poetry and music.

Apollo agreed to a contest, which was to be judged by Tmolus, the mountain-god, and the foolhardy Midas of the Golden Touch, by now king of Phrygia. Whoever won was to choose whatever punishment he wished for the loser.

The first to play was Babys, on his single pipe, but the squeaks and whines he emitted were so laughable that he was eliminated from the challenge, leaving only Marsyas facing Apollo.

Marsyas picked up his flute and the airs he played were so beautiful that all the birds and the bees stopped to listen. Apollo picked up his lyre and the melodies he played were so beautiful that the clouds came down from the sky to hear them.

The judges declared a tie and, to break it, ordered Marsyas to play his flute upside down. Even Marsyas could not produce a tune under such conditions, and Tmolus proclaimed Apollo the winner.

'Fool!' cried Midas, forgetting the trouble that loose words had caused him the last time. 'Where are your ears? Can you not hear that Marsyas is still the better player?'

But Tmolus was already placing the victor's laurel wreath on Apollo's head.

Now Apollo, in cruel revenge, claimed his prize, imposing hideous punishments on Marsyas. Soon bored with his game, however, he relented and changed his victim into a stream instead.

Then Apollo turned his attention to Midas.

'Where are your ears, you ask. Well, look to your own …'

And as Midas touched his ears, he felt them changing, becoming broader, longer, pointed, hairy.

Apollo had transformed his ears into those of an ass.

Midas fled in shame, and from that day on, always wore a Phrygian cap on his head to conceal his secret.

But there was one person who knew the secret – the palace barber who cut the king's hair, and who was made to swear, that he would never divulge what he knew to any living thing.

Now a secret unshared is a terrible burden, and in the end the barber could bear it no longer. If he could not tell any living thing, then he would tell the ground on which he stood. So he went out beyond the palace walls, and there he dug a hole in the ground, and whispered into it:

'King Midas has ass's ears …' after which he felt a lot better.

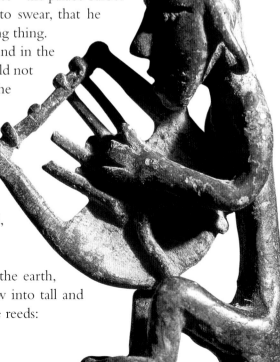

Summer came, then winter, then spring, and all the time the hole lay there in the ground, silent and guarding its secret:

'King Midas has ass's ears …'

And the soft spring rain fell and moistened the earth, and little shoots appeared in the hole, and grew into tall and slender reeds, and the hole gave its secret to the reeds:

'King Midas has ass's ears …'

Then the gentle wind came and caressed the reeds and ran its fingers through them like a lover through his beloved's hair, and the reeds whispered their secret to the wind:

'King Midas has ass's ears ...'

And the wind picked up the secret and carried it on its wide wings to all the places where it blew, north, south, east, and west, so that in the end the whole world knew what the king had tried so hard to conceal:

'King Midas has ass's ears ... King Midas has ass's ears ...'

THE HUNTER AND THE MOON GODDESS

Actæon, son of Aristaeus and Autonoë, liked nothing so much as hunting. With his pack of fifty hounds – white-bodied and red-eared – he roamed all the forests and mountains in pursuit of game.

One fine day, a particularly magnificent stag presented itself and Actæon gave chase. The beast led him and his hounds a merry dance, up and down hills, over stony pathways, through thickets and across streams until, with a mighty bound, it leapt over a ravine and disappeared where neither hunter nor pack could follow.

In the heat of the chase, Actæon had wandered far beyond his accustomed territory and now found himself in the midst of a mountain glade. With his hounds milling and snuffling around his feet, he stood still and looked about him.

Chestnut and oak trees soared above his head, making a broken patchwork of leaves pierced by slivers of sky. A flickering pattern of light played over trunks and branches and dappled the forest floor with dancing shadows. The air was fragrant with the smell of damp leaves and sweet violets. All was hushed and silent, except for the occasional rush of a bird's wings or the rustle of animals in the undergrowth. But the forest is a mysterious place, with enchantments and bewitcheries at every turn, and in its very quietness, it was as if the forest was waiting ...

As Actæon listened in the silence, he thought he heard the sound of gently rippling water coming from some distance away. There was something else, too: the sound of tinkling laughter.

Like the skilful hunter that he was, Actæon crept stealthily in the direction of the laughter, taking care where he placed his foot lest the crack of a breaking twig should announce his presence. He reached the edge of the glade and then, what a sight met his eyes!

In a small clearing ahead of him a broad stream bubbled; on its banks lay a saffron tunic with a red hem, and on this rested a silver bow and a quiverful of arrows; and in the ripples of the stream a large group of nymphs were dipping themselves, splashing and laughing. All the nymphs were young and beautiful, but one in the middle – taller than the rest – surpassed all the others in her splendour. Her face was oval, her naked skin was moon-white and she wore a silver crescent in her hair. She was the Maiden of the Silver Bow, the Lady of the Beasts, the Mistress of Moonlight, the Goddess of the Chase: Actæon was looking on Artemis herself.

He was entranced; he could not take his eyes off her. He stayed to watch, resting his back against a large boulder where – or so he thought – he was hidden from view. But Artemis saw him as he watched her at her bath, and in her steady gaze the hunter felt a strange change come over him.

His nose lengthened, his forehead flattened, and his neck thickened. His shoulders shrank back and his trunk became broad and muscular. His ears grew long and pointed and antlers

sprouted from his head. Where once was a nose was now a muzzle. Where once were arms, there now were legs. Where once were feet, there now were hooves.

The hunter had become the hunted – Actæon had changed into a stag.

And now Artemis turned her steady gaze on his hounds, who had come padding after their master. The dogs raised their noses and sniffed the air, as if scenting a new quarry; they began to bark and howl – and then they spotted Actæon …

'Wait!' cried Actæon from within his stag's body as the pack advanced towards him. 'Wait, Melampus and Ichnobates, Pterelas, Theras and Hylaeus … wait!' he cried, calling them all by name. 'I am your master – do you not know me?'

But no human voice came from his throat, only a stag's cry drowned by the baying of the hounds. Driven by an instinct bred deep in their marrow, the pack had only one impulse – to kill.

It was in a copse on the other side of the hill that they finally brought him down, pulling at hair and limb and muscle as he writhed in the convulsions of death, tearing his body apart in the lust of slaughter and devouring the warm, still-pulsating flesh. What a kill the dogs had that day …

And when they had finally finished with him, the goddess was at last appeased and nature covered over all signs of his existence, like the leaves that blanket the grave. The birds sang in the branches again, the trees rustled in the breeze, the brook and the broad stream continued, as they had always done, on their babbling way down to the sea, and all was peaceful once more in the forests and mountains where Artemis reigned.

The Pride of Arachne

Between north and south, between east and west, mountains and sea, in a land called Lydia, there once lived a young woman by the name of Arachne.

Arachne was of humble parentage, her father being a dyer of cloth in the rich purples extracted from shellfish caught in the blue Aegean Sea. Perhaps it was these gorgeous colourings that inspired her, or perhaps it was a talent born in her bones, none can say for sure, but all agreed – no one could weave like Arachne.

All day long she would sit at her loom, its rhythmic clickety-clack ruffling the sleepy air as the shuttle flew back and forth, locking weft into warp in tapestries of the most exquisite perfection. With nothing more than the yarns at her fingertips, Arachne wove pictures as fine as those of any great artist. Here was blossom real enough to fool the bees, and birds ready to leap into flight; here were perfumed meadows, and rivers with swimming fish; here were boats bobbing on a white-crested blue sea, and fishermen in the boats casting their nets, and villages clinging to cliffsides, and temples and palaces, and mountains that scraped the heavens, and deep, stream-spangled valleys. All of life was in Arachne's tapestries. It was as if the scenes she showed had lain dormant in the threads, waiting only for her touch to reveal themselves.

Of course, Arachne's fame quickly spread and everyone from her own village and all the villages around came to watch her at work. What whispered admirings rose from the murmuring crowd with each new run of the shuttle, as the onlookers jostled for a better view of the creation that was coming to life, before their eyes, on Arachne's loom.

Naturally, the weaver herself did not remain unmoved by such adulation. As the days wore on, a definite air of smugness settled on her face. There was no one in the whole world, she thought to herself, who was her equal in the craft of weaving. She could even, she ventured to think, say that there was not her equal in heaven. Oh, there was nothing as satisfying as being better than everyone else! The thought wrapped itself around her and warmed her like a fur cloak on a winter's night.

Up on cloud-capped Olympus, Athene, goddess of weaving, had been watching all these goings-on, down near the shores of the Aegean Sea. She had seen the streams of people walking back and forth, like columns of black ants, from Arachne's house, talking excitedly to each other. 'What colours! What artistry! Have you ever seen weaving so fine? The girl's a genius …'

Athene decided to come down from heaven and see this paragon for herself. Naturally, she took the precaution of not appearing as herself. She came instead as an old woman, feeble of limb and bent of back, wearing an old grey cloak and leaning on a stick. Undetected, she joined the throng. She made her way to the front.

Arachne was, at this time, feeling particularly pleased with herself. She had just executed her most ambitious work yet, a vast tapestry that told in episodic scenes the whole story of her own country, Lydia. It was an impressive piece.

Athene stepped forward.

'My dear child, you have a prodigious talent. Surely you must have learned your gift from the great Athene herself?'

'Grandmother, your ancient brain is as feeble as your body … what witless ramblings you spew! Be off with you, old rickety-bones. I owe Athene nothing – just let her come here herself and I'll show her who is the better craftswoman!'

'Oh, but she *is* here,' said Athene as her cloak fell from her to reveal the goddess in all her tall and stately radiance.

Arachne could not retract the challenge so hastily uttered, and a second loom was brought. Athene set to, and began weaving. Her fingers flew, the shuttle whizzed, and a picture began to emerge. It showed all the mortals who had been impudent enough to challenge the gods, and the punishments they had earned. Arachne set to, and began weaving. Her fingers flew, the shuttle whizzed, and a quite different picture began to emerge. It showed all the indiscretions of the gods. There was Zeus, disguised as a bull, a swan, a cloud, a shower of gold, in lustful pursuit of this or that woman. There was his brother Poseidon, similarly disguised and engaged, and Apollo, too. The gods were exposed for the seducers and libertines that they really were.

These, then, were the scenes presented in the tapestries of the goddess and the girl. But in the judging of the stitchery, there was not a hair's breadth between the skill of the one and the other. In every detail, Arachne's weaving was as fine as that of Athene.

Enraged at being so well matched, and furious that members of her own family should be depicted in this disrespectful way, Athene raised her staff and struck Arachne on the forehead, and Arachne vanished.

But down on the floor, where she had only a moment before stood, a tiny creature was seen scuttling away towards a dark corner. It had a small, round, black body and eight nimble little legs. It was Arachne, metamorphosed. The spinner had become the spider.

From that day on, Arachne never ceased her toil, doomed as she was to weave forever with the thread that she draws from her own body. Look into any dark corner or hidden place, and you might find her. She goes by a new name now. She is known as an arachnid, in memory of the girl she once was. Her webs are the finest you have ever seen, suspended like fairy lace between window and wall and stem and branch. When one is broken, by the wind or a careless hand, she untiringly takes up the yarn once more, an airborne acrobat launching herself into space to construct again her silken wheel. And if she has not died, she is weaving still.

THE WHITE MOON COW

Long, long ago, in southern Greece, there lived a priestess of the moon by the name of Io. Io tended the shrine of the Heraion, and was the representative on earth of holy, cow-eyed Hera.

One day, while she was going about her sacred duties, Zeus the bull-god looked down from his pinnacle in heaven to see what he might see … and what he saw was Io. The moment he saw her, he wanted her, and what he wanted, he took.

To achieve his end, however, Zeus knew that a degree of guile was necessary if his wife Hera was not to be alerted to his plan. So, in order to reach the lovely Io undetected, he changed himself into a cloud, and drifted down to earth, where he caught her in his vaporous embrace and veiled her from all eyes. Within the blanketing cloud, Io was transformed, too. She became a white cow, with flanks as pale as the silver moon and horns the shape of a crescent. And in this bovine guise, she gave way to the seductions of the bull-god who had come to her in the midst of the mist.

When the mist was gone and the sky was again clear, Hera looked down from her pinnacle in heaven to see what she might see … and what she saw was a pretty white cow, with pearly flanks and crescent horns, grazing where no cattle had been before, near the shrine of the Heraion.

She knew at once what had happened.

'That white moon-cow is mine,' she said to Zeus – which, of course, was true, since the beast had formerly been one of her priestesses. With each knowing that the other knew but neither prepared to speak it, Zeus, in silent complicity with the shared pretence, handed over the pretty little heifer to his wife, as a gift.

To prevent any further infidelity on the part of her husband, Hera immediately placed her new acquisition under the guardianship of Argos *Panoptes* – 'he who sees all' – a giant with one hundred eyes, only fifty of which were ever closed in sleep while the other fifty remained watchfully open.

But in the game of wits called marriage there is always another card to play, and this time it belonged to Zeus. The bull-god sent Hermes, messenger of the gods, to sit by Argos and enchant him with the music of his magic flute.

'Greetings, friend,' said Hermes as he lowered himself down beside Argos. 'This cowherding is a boring business – allow me to entertain you with a little tune, to pass the time …'

And as Hermes started to play, an irresistible drowsiness overcame the unsuspecting Argos. Fifty of his eyes were already shut – what harm would it do to shut just one more, he thought. That would still leave forty-nine on duty. The lid of his fifty-first eye became heavy, quivered, lowered, and shut. Soon the same affliction affected his fifty-second eye, then his fifty-third, then his fifty-fourth. Now only forty eyes were open, now thirty, now twenty, now ten, now none. Argos was fast asleep, in a delicious slumber as deep as a baby's.

Hermes at once set to work. He cut off the giant's head, and allowed Io, still disguised as a cow, to make good her escape.

When Hera discovered that she had been outwitted, she was furious. In rage at her watchman's gullibility, she tore out all of his one hundred eyes and tossed them into the tail of her favourite peacock, where they still wink and blink to this day.

As for the unfortunate Io, Hera sent after her a stinging insect – a gadfly – to pursue her across the world, to harass her and bite her and suck her blood. And so Io the *tauropárthenos*, the 'virgin dedicated to the bull', was forced to flee.

In crazed torment, she plunged into the sea, and with the buzzing and nipping of her tormentor ever spurring her on, began her circuitous journey. She crossed and criss-crossed the world in wide circles like the moon that crosses the heavens, going now west to the sea, to the Ionian that bears her name, now northeast to the Black Sea and Bosphorus, now southward through Phoenicia and east to Bactria and India, now southwest to Arabia and Ethiopia, onward, ever onward in her desperation to escape what she could not, until finally, defeated, she sank all but lifeless onto the soil of Egypt. Here Zeus at last released her from her torment, skimming his hand over her like the breeze that skims the treetops, and returning her to human form. Io stayed on in Egypt, and gave birth to a son whom she called Epaphus, which means 'a hand's light touch'. But some say that he was also Apis, the bull-god of Egypt, child of a white moon-cow and a bull-god who appeared in the midst of a mist.

THE SACRED MARRIAGE

In many Greek myths, we see the pairing of a female and a male in the guise of a horned animal. The most famous are probably those that belong to the Minotaur cycle (see pages 107–15) – Zeus the bull and Europa, the bull of Poseidon and Pasiphaë the 'cow', Dionysos the bull and Ariadne – but there are also Zeus and Io the white cow, and Actæon the stag and Artemis. Looking through the narrative of these myths to the message beneath, we see the image of the 'sacred marriage'. This was an ancient rite, pre-dating Classical Greece, to renew the king's sacred powers and the life-force he embodied through ritual 'marriage' to the source of his power, the goddess, and ritual sacrifice. The ceremony of marriage would have been enacted by a priest and priestess in the roles of king and goddess-queen, dressed in the masks and costumes of a bull and cow (or perhaps a stag and a hind). The story of Pasiphaë, who wore a cow costume to seduce a bull, and the Minotaur, who had the body of a man and the 'head' – or mask – of a bull both evoke this custom, as do Io who was 'changed' into a cow, and Actæon 'changed' into a stag.

As to the ritual sacrifice, this would originally, it is believed, have involved the real king himself but later a surrogate animal – often a bull – took his place. The death of the Athenians at the hands of the bull-man was a kind of sacrifice by proxy.

But behind these ritual elements there is an even deeper symbolism. The timing of the sacred marriage which renewed the power of the king may well have corresponded to the moment every eight years when the Sun and Moon 'come together', when the solar and lunar cycles coincide (the Athenian sacrifice to the Minotaur occurred on an eight-yearly cycle). Thus the bull (or stag) comes to represent the power of the Sun, and the cow (or hind) the Moon. 'Wide-eyed' Europa, 'all-illuminating' Pasiphaë, Ariadne the 'one who shines from afar', Io the priestess of the Moon in service to 'cow-eyed Hera' all have lunar allusions. In the story of Actæon, Artemis quite openly is the Moon, while her admirer, in the guise of a stag, suffers the sacrificial fate of kings when he is killed by his own hounds at the Moon's instigation.

Love and Loss

ORPHEUS AND EURYDICE

ORPHEUS WAS THE GREATEST musician and poet who has ever lived. His mother was Calliope, the Muse who inspired epic poetry, and his father was the Thracian king Oegrus. Others, however, maintained that his real father was Apollo, god of music and poetry, but there was one point on which all were agreed: it was Apollo who had given Orpheus his lyre.

The music that Orpheus played on this instrument was unlike any other. When he lifted his lyre and ran his fingers across its strings, the sound he made was like the bubbling of a brook over stones, like the coo-cooing of turtle doves in the eaves, like the melody of the skylark in the wide blue heaven, like the song of the waves caressing the shore, like the siren-call of the mermaids from the deep, for the tunes he played came from the deepest places of the heart and they dripped from his strings like honey from a spoon.

So prodigious was his talent that his music had the power to reverse the natural order of things. When Orpheus sat in a clearing in the woods and picked up his lyre and played, all the wild beasts, red in tooth and claw, were lulled to stillness and listened, predator alongside prey. The mountaintops bowed their heads in order to hear more clearly, and even rocks and trees uprooted themselves from where they stood and clustered around him. Then the wizard musician, the divine bard, would lead the throng in the dance. Bewitched by his music of enchantment, lions, lambs, wolves, goats, stags and wild horses; eagles, crows and sparrows; pebbles, stones and boulders; laurels, acacias, cypresses and oaks; all these and many more found themselves compelled to move in time to the ripple and rhythm of the strings, to dip, to whirl, to spin, to caper, to dance in an undulating line that swayed back and forth like the ebb and swell of the sea. Indeed, there is a site in Thrace where to this very day the mountain oaks still stand where Orpheus left them, in the pattern of the dance.

Now in the groves and wild places where Orpheus made his music there lived numerous nymphs, and one of them was called Eurydice. Orpheus loved Eurydice passionately and she became his wife. The joy he felt in his love he expressed in his music, and his songs now were so beautiful that the very stars in heaven danced.

But even for one such as Orpheus, happiness was not to last. One day, when Eurydice was wandering alone in the valley of the river Peneios, a villain by the name of Aristaeos tried to violate her. In her frightened flight from him, she inadvertently stepped on a snake who injected its fatal venom into her ankle, and she died instantly. Like so many before and since, she was at once transported to the kingdom of Hades below the earth, where she became one of the Shades, the ghostly host of the dead.

Orpheus looked everywhere for his beloved and, when he could not find her, the horrible realization of what must have happened dawned on him. She was dead! He was beside himself with grief. She was his love, she was life itself. How could he go on without her? All around him a heartless world continued the daily business of existence. The sun still shone in the sky, the birds still sang, the flowers still bloomed, but without Eurydice everything was meaningless.

The pain of her loss was almost more than it was possible to bear, and he took up his lyre once more in an attempt to console himself. As the limpid notes floated from the strings, an idea gradually began to take shape in Orpheus' mind. If his music had the power to enchant the birds and the beasts, the rocks and the trees, might it not have the power to charm Hades, god of the underworld, too?

And so the son of shining Apollo set off, not to sing for his supper like any ordinary minstrel, but to sing a song that would melt the heart of the king of the dead and in so doing earn the release of his beloved.

Down, down, deep into the earth he went, and what a dark and desolate journey it was. He passed through the Grove of Persephone, where black poplars and sterile willows grow; he fed a honey cake to Cerberus, three-headed watchdog of hell; he saw the streams of death, that flow like rivers of tears through the underworld – the Acheron, the river of affliction, the Cocytus, the river of lamentation, the Lethe, river of forgetfulness, and the Styx, that winds its course nine times around the dark kingdom. He travelled in the boat of Charon the ferryman and, finally, he arrived at his destination: he was in the presence of Hades and his queen, Persephone.

It was then that he picked up his lyre and lifted his voice and began to sing, and his song was of such poignant beauty that it would have broken your heart if you had been there to hear it. As the strains of his music wafted through the subterranean chambers of Hades' kingdom, even the torments of Hell suffered by the Shades were temporarily suspended, as if time itself had been arrested and hung in the air like frozen breath. Tantalus stopped trying to quench his thirst in the lake that shrank from him every time he stooped to drink. Sisyphus stopped trying to push a rock up a hill only to have it roll down again as soon as he had reached the top. And the Danaids stopped trying to fill a broken jar with water from a sieve.

When Orpheus finally laid down his lyre, there was a hush throughout the halls of hell for what seemed like an eternity. Then Hades spoke:

'You may take Eurydice back with you, but on one condition. You must not turn around to look at her until you both stand once more in the realm of sunlight.'

This seemed an easy enough condition, and Orpheus eagerly agreed to the terms laid before him. He began the journey home, in the sure knowledge that Eurydice was following close behind. They went back by the same way he had come – back past Cerberus, back over the water with Charon, back through the grove of lifeless trees. And all the while Orpheus played on his lyre, its music acting like a thread of sound leading them up to the light.

They were approaching the exit now. Orpheus could see a glimmer of sunlight. Soon he would hold Eurydice in his arms again. He could hardly wait.

He touched his foot on the threshold of the upper world. He had done it! They were home! They were free, and he had saved his Eurydice from death. Just to make sure she was still behind him – and just to see her beautiful face that he had dared not look on up until now – he turned around, only to see a distraught Eurydice holding out her arms to him as she faded, faded, faded from view, swallowed back into the maw of the grave. In his eagerness, Orpheus had been too hasty. He had looked back too soon, before his beloved was also out in the light, and he had paid the price.

Eurydice was lost to him for ever, and he grieved sorely for the rest of his days. All the joy went from his song and he became as a ghost, haunting all the wild and lonely places of the mountains. For seven months after his return from the underworld, people said they could still hear the faint strains of his mournful lyre, floating down to them on the breeze. But others said no, it was only the howl of the north wind as it roamed the distant gorges, gullies and peaks.

After a time, even these sounds were stilled, and it was rumoured that Orpheus had killed himself. But the truth was even crueller. Orpheus died at the hands of the Maenads, wild women in the service of Dionysos, who tore him limb from bleeding limb in an ecstacy of rage, because the bard had failed to show due respect to their lord.

When they ripped his head from his body it was still singing, and they threw it into the river Hebrus, on which it floated its slow course down to the sea, singing all the while. The Maenads, meanwhile, attempted to wash away their victim's blood in the waters of the river Helicorn, but the river-god dived below the earth to emerge some miles distant, and under another name – Baphyra – to avoid being an ally in murder.

When the head of Orpheus reached the sea, it continued its journey, carried on the current, still singing, singing, singing, and the airs it sang were so plaintive and beautiful that the fishermen in their little boats stopped to listen, believing that they heard the song of mermaids, and the sea-birds ceased their crying. At last, the singing head arrived at the island of Lesbos, where it became lodged in a rock, but was later moved to a sacred cave at Antissa on the northern shores of the island, and here for many a long year it continued to utter, dispensing wisdom and pronouncing oracular truths.

The magical lyre similarly drifted to Lesbos where it was placed in a temple of Apollo but later, at the insistence of the god and the Muses, was borne up to the heavens where it took its place amongst the stars.

As for the bard's mutilated body and severed and scattered limbs, the Muses patiently collected them together and took them to Leibethra, at the foot of Mount Olympus, where they laid them in the earth, with much weeping and lamentation. And to this very day, it is said that in that place, where the bones of Orpheus lie buried, the nightingales sing more sweetly than anywhere else in Greece.

PHILEMON AND BAUCIS

Once upon a time, there lived an old man and an old woman called Philemon and Baucis. They had been married for many a year, and none was a year too long for they loved each other dearly. Their home was a humble cottage in a village in a shallow, wooded valley, and here the two elderly peasants lived a simple life. Although they were poor, they were content for they had each other, and they did not hanker for the wealth they had never known.

Behind the cottage was a little plot partly shaded by the silvery leaves and gnarled branches of a large olive tree. Here some vines grew and a few rows of beans. A tethered goat, from whose milk Baucis made a soft, white cheese, grazed on the rough grass, a pig snortled in the leaf litter, and a couple of chickens pecked on the ground for such insect titbits as they might find.

Now throughout the ancient world, there was a well-known rule, that whenever a weary traveller knocked on a stranger's door asking for shelter he should be treated as a guest and offered the hospitality of the home – food to eat, wine, beer or mead to drink, and a bed for the night. But in the village where Philemon and Baucis lived, no one – apart from the old couple themselves – seemed to acknowledge this unwritten law, so that when a traveller came knocking he would be greeted with such words of welcome as 'Be off with you! Do you think I have enough food to feed every passing beggar? On your way, or I'll set the dogs on you!' And the door would be resolutely slammed in the visitor's open-mouthed face.

One searingly blue day, when the sun was so hot that you had to shield your eyes just to gaze ahead of you and the only relief was in whatever shade could be found, a pair of strangers were seen approaching the village, along the dusty path that led down into the valley.

Their approach was closely observed by the inhabitants of the village, who always seemed to take the greatest exception to any potential threat to their familiar daily routine, and would resist it with all the rudeness at their command. As the strangers came level with the first few cottages, backs were turned, engrossing conversations suddenly sprang up which brooked no interruption, and doors were loudly and pointedly slammed. Clearly, there was no welcome to be had here.

Looking tired and grubby from what must have been a long march, the two strangers trudged on until, as the cluster of cottages thinned, they arrived at last at the one belonging to Philemon and Baucis.

Baucis was sitting on the front step, shelling beans and arranging them on a tray for drying. As soon as she spotted the travellers, she laid down her work, jumped to her feet, and rushed over to them.

'Come! Come!' she said, stretching out her thin old hands to them. 'Welcome to our humble home. Please come inside and rest and take some refreshment. You look quite worn out!'

By this time, Philemon had arrived, alerted by his wife's noisy greeting, and the pair ushered their visitors solicitously inside. While Philemon gathered sticks and built up the fire for cooking, Baucis busied herself preparing a meal. Into the pot she threw beans, garlic, and pieces of salt bacon. On a rough terracotta dish she placed a chunk of cheese, some olives, a handful of herbs, some eggs roasted in the embers of the fire, and a flat round of coarse bread, lightly sprinkled with oil from the olives. Next to this she set a flagon of wine, made from the grapes in her own small garden.

This was indeed a feast fit for the gods, and far more than the frugal fare that she and her husband would have had if eating alone. The food set out before their guests would probably, under normal circumstances, have fed the couple for one or two weeks, but then, unlike their fellow villagers, Philemon and Baucis knew how to welcome strangers.

Hosts and guests settled down to enjoy their meal, but hardly had they begun than a very strange thing happened. As the wine flagon was passed from one to the other and its contents drunk, it remained as full as it had been at the outset, no matter how much was taken from it. Philemon and Baucis had heard tell of such wonders, of horns of plenty that were always full of whatever foods their owners wished for. But such marvels belonged to gods, not to humans, and seeing their familiar flagon performing magical tricks before their very eyes was highly disturbing.

It was then that they began to wonder about the true identity of their guests. They stole glances at the two strangers who had chosen to shelter under their roof. One had a particularly majestic air, even though he was cloaked in the roughly woven garb of a traveller. Was it just a trick of the light, or were those really glints of fire sparkling through the coarse, open weave of his clothing? As for the other, closer examination revealed curious sandals with wings on them, as if the wearer were some sky-traveller from the otherworld.

Reality gradually dawned. The strangers whom Philemon and Baucis had so generously entertained were not mortals, but gods.

'Yes, you are right,' said the majestic one, who seemed to have the ability to mind-read. 'We are gods. I am Zeus, and this …' indicating his companion, 'is Hermes.'

'Oh, your greatnesses, oh, your majesties, we are deeply honoured, deeply flattered …' Philemon and Baucis stuttered and fumbled for the words to convey their awe.

'And now,' Zeus continued, 'I want you to come with us.' And the two gods led the old couple up a hill that overlooked the village and the valley. By now it was evening, and a full moon shone in a turquoise and cobalt sky.

'There …' said Zeus, pointing at the rooftops below, 'there live people whose only concern is for themselves, who turn their backs on pleas for shelter and warmth, who would leave others out in the blackness of night where they are prey to hunger, cold, and wolves rather than open their doors to them. There live people who must pay the consequences of their actions.'

As Philemon and Baucis watched, all the cottages began to sink beneath a rising flood of water that became a wide lake, shining like a sheet of silver in the moonlight, which looked as if it had been there for all eternity. The only cottage which remained standing was theirs, and this too began to change.

The cracked and crumbling walls grew tall and smooth and white, and the reeds of the thatch glittered in the moon's cool rays. The place where they had once lived had become a magnificent temple, with walls of marble and roof of gold.

'For your kindness and goodness, I will grant you one wish,' said Zeus. 'What is it you wish for?'

Philemon and Baucis looked at each other. There was no need to ask.

'What we would like,' they said, 'is for us both to die at the same time, so that neither one is left to grieve for the other.'

'Take it as done,' said Zeus.

The couple returned to their former home, where they lived as priest and priestess of the new temple until they grew so enfeebled that their backs were bent, their eyes clouded with the milkiness of age, their hair thin and fine as goosedown, and they tottered with a tentative gait, leaning on sticks for support.

One day, a peasant came up to the temple bearing a gift of new-laid eggs for the ancient pair, but Philemon and Baucis were nowhere to be found. Instead, just in front of the door two trees stood, an oak and a lime, where no trees had stood before, and their branches were so interlaced that you could not tell where one ended and the other began. The oak was Philemon and the lime was Baucis, together in death as they had been in life, with their arms entwined in a loving embrace.

For centuries, even after the temple had fallen to ruins, the trees still stood, offering their hospitable shade to travellers who stopped to rest awhile beneath them. The legend of how they had come to be was now famous, and the travellers, sitting in their softly dappled shelter, took pleasure in recounting the ancient tale to each other.

'Once upon a time,' they would begin, 'there lived an old man and an old woman called Philemon and Baucis. They had been married for many a year, and none was a year too long for they loved each other dearly …'

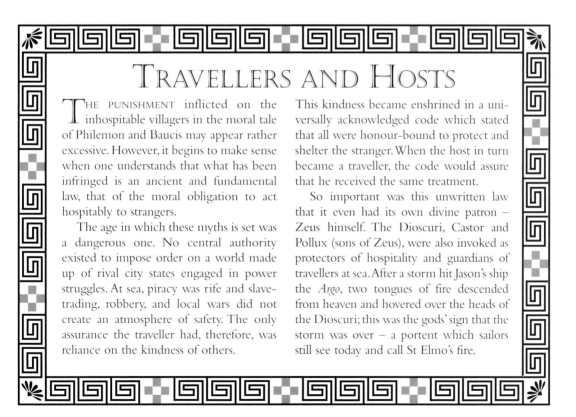

TRAVELLERS AND HOSTS

THE PUNISHMENT inflicted on the inhospitable villagers in the moral tale of Philemon and Baucis may appear rather excessive. However, it begins to make sense when one understands that what has been infringed is an ancient and fundamental law, that of the moral obligation to act hospitably to strangers.

The age in which these myths is set was a dangerous one. No central authority existed to impose order on a world made up of rival city states engaged in power struggles. At sea, piracy was rife and slave-trading, robbery, and local wars did not create an atmosphere of safety. The only assurance the traveller had, therefore, was reliance on the kindness of others.

This kindness became enshrined in a universally acknowledged code which stated that all were honour-bound to protect and shelter the stranger. When the host in turn became a traveller, the code would assure that he received the same treatment.

So important was this unwritten law that it even had its own divine patron – Zeus himself. The Dioscuri, Castor and Pollux (sons of Zeus), were also invoked as protectors of hospitality and guardians of travellers at sea. After a storm hit Jason's ship the *Argo*, two tongues of fire descended from heaven and hovered over the heads of the Dioscuri; this was the gods' sign that the storm was over – a portent which sailors still see today and call St Elmo's fire.

PYGMALION AND GALATEA

Long, long ago, on an island whose shores were washed by an aquamarine sea, whose hills were mottled with scrub and baked to a golden crust by a fierce sun, whose nights were soft as black velvet encrusted with the diamond-points of a myriad of stars, there lived a king. His name was Pygmalion and the island was Cyprus, and it belonged to the love goddess Aphrodite who had reached it by bobbing across the waves in a boat made of a sea-shell.

Pygmalion had no queen. This was not because of a shortage of candidates, for there were plenty of women of rank and beauty from whom he could have chosen. The fact was that Pygmalion was already in love but the one woman he wanted in all the world was the one woman he could not have. That woman was Aphrodite.

'Why will you not lie with me, oh heartless one?' he wailed to her. 'There are other men on whom you have bestowed your favours – why not me?'

But despite his entreaties, Aphrodite remained tantalizingly, alluring and frustratingly distant.

Pygmalion did not know what to do. His love and longing for the love goddess was making him ill. He could not eat, he could not sleep – he was a man lost in a mist of misery. No matter how inventive, how increasingly imaginative the palace cook's creations were, still the king refused to partake of anything but the smallest morsels. Haggard-eyed and hollow-cheeked, he wandered the palace halls like a ghost. Clearly, his kingship was no defence against maladies of the heart, to which monarchs and paupers are equal prey. Like a boy in the pangs of sexual awakening, Pygmalion was, in short, horribly lovesick.

The king decided that if he could not possess the object of his desires, then he must have her image. So he set to work with chisel and blade and fashioned an exact, life-size replica of Aphrodite in ivory. The statue was identical to the goddess in every physical detail. The arch of her eyebrow, the gentle sweep of her nose, the slope of her shoulders, the swell of her breasts and buttocks, the curve of her thigh, the delicate line of her ankle; all were modelled to perfection, for who after all would know such details so well as one who worshipped her as passionately as Pygmalion?

The ivory statue gave the king relief from his anguish for a time. He would not be parted from it and – I am ashamed to say – even took it to bed with him, where he would embrace and caress its cool curves and smooth planes in the hope that somehow the inanimate form lying next to him would respond.

But it was no use. The beautiful, statue remained as icily unmoved as the cold ivory from which it was made.

'Have pity on me!' Pygmalion prayed to Aphrodite. 'You see how I suffer. Even your image affords me no comfort. I am cursed by love. Release me from this bondage or I think I shall die!' And he turned to the statue by his side, put his arms despairingly around it, and sobbed as if his heart would break.

His tears fell on the statue's cheek and ran in little rivulets down its breast, and then something strange and miraculous happened. As if in answer to Pygmalion's weeping, a small, perfect, oval dew-drop issued from the corner of one of the ivory figure's eyes and rolled slowly down the side of its exquisite nose. The statue was crying. Aphrodite, hearing Pygmalion's prayer, had invisibly entered her ivory twin and had breathed life into it.

Awkwardly, the statue raised her arms and cradled Pygmalion's head. The flesh that was once as cool and unyielding as stone now exuded warmth and life. The cheeks that were once pearl-pale were now flushed with rose. The lips that were once silent now spoke.

'My name is Galatea,' the statue said to an amazed Pygmalion.

Well, the rest of the story is as you might expect. Pygmalion married Galatea, and now that he had a real flesh-and-blood Aphrodite of his own he no longer yearned for the divine original, and his appetite and zest for life improved immeasurably.

In time, Galatea bore Pygmalion a son by the name of Paphos, who in turn had a son called Cinyras who founded the Cyprian city of Paphos, named after his father, and there built a famous temple to Aphrodite, without whose kindness neither he nor his father would ever have been born.

So ends the tale of Pygmalion and his Galatea, which began sadly but ended happily, as we hope all good stories will.

THE THEFT OF PERSEPHONE

Once, in a golden age long, long ago, when there were neither cold nor storms nor snow nor ice, mortals basked in an endless summer. Food was there for the taking – luscious fruits hung from the branches, rich, ripe corn waved in the fields, and fat sheep and cows with udders bursting with creamy milk grazed in lush meadows. But such happy times were not to last, for one day, a misfortune befell the daughter of Demeter, and it was this that first brought winter to the world.

With hair the colour of ripened corn, Demeter was goddess of the fertile land, and the fruitfulness of the world

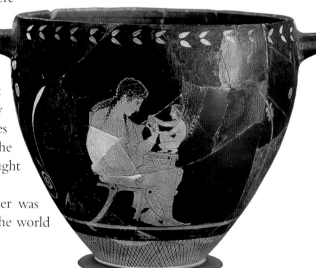

was hers to command. The name of her daughter was Kore, a maiden as fresh and fair as the blossom on the trees in spring. One day, Kore was out in the meadows gathering wild flowers when she noticed a narcissus of particular beauty. Innocently, she stooped to pick it, and as she did so, it was as if she had turned a key and opened a door into the belly of the earth, for at once a deep rumbling was heard from below, the earth began to shake and shiver and – as she watched, frozen with fear – a huge chasm opened before her. Out of it thundered a dark chariot, pulled by dark horses, and in the dark chariot was Hades, Lord of the Underworld. Before Kore had a chance to cry out for help, Hades seized her, placed her beside him, and bore her off to his underworld kingdom. As the chariot whirled out of sight, the wound that it had opened in the earth closed over and all was as peaceful as before, with no sign that anything had ever been amiss.

When Demeter came searching for her daughter and could not find her, it was as if all light and life had gone out of the world. Flinging over her shoulder the sombre veil of sorrow, the goddess flew like a bird over land and sea, seeking her lost child. When at last she discovered the name of the thief – and worse still, that Zeus, lord of the gods and brother to Hades, had conspired in the crime – she was beyond herself with rage and despair. She disguised herself as an old woman, and desolately wandered the world of man looking for her daughter. At last she arrived at Eleusis, kingdom of the wise Celeus, in Attica. No one guessed the goddess's true identity, and in the king's palace she became nurse to his infant son.

She tended the boy with care and decided that she would confer on him the greatest gift of all, that of immortality, and so began the magical process of transformation. Instead of giving the child food, she breathed on him and anointed him with divine ambrosia and

placed him in the coals of the fire at night to burn away his mortality, and day by day the boy became more and more god-like.

The boy's mother Metaneira noticed a change in her son and, suspicious, decided to spy on the old nurse to see if she could discover the cause. When she saw her lowering the boy into the fire and apparently trying to burn him to death, she screamed in horror, whereupon the goddess turned and told her that, had it not been for her interference, her son would have become immortal. Demeter now revealed her true identity and, with all the divine majesty at her command, ordered that a temple be built for her in Eleusis, where the people might come to celebrate her mysteries. This was done, and for many a long year the Eleusinian Mysteries were performed there by her initiates.

In gratitude to Celeus' family for their hospitality, Demeter also imparted to their oldest son, Triptolemus, her secrets. It was Triptolemus to whom she gave the first grain of corn, and taught him how to sow it and husband it and harvest it so that humankind would for ever have the power to feed themselves. It was Triptolemus whom she showed how to harness oxen to the plough to ease the work of the farmer. It was Triptolemus to whom she gave a winged chariot drawn by dragons that he might travel the world spreading knowledge among all men of the boons she had given him.

But all that was yet to come, for the goddess had other matters to attend to first. Seated in her temple at Eleusis, Demeter vowed revenge for the theft of her daughter, and it was a terrible revenge indeed, for she placed a curse on the land, saying that it would not bear any fruit until Kore was returned to her. And so it was. For the first time since man and beast had walked the earth, the corn would not grow, the fruit would not ripen, and

cold and darkness, famine and death spread their affliction over the world. Every creature, every mortal was struck with a terrible and biting hunger.

In desperation, Zeus sent the rainbow-goddess Iris to plead with Demeter. Descending to Earth on her iridescent bridge, Iris begged the goddess to relent, but it was of no use. One by one, other gods came, but still Demeter was determined and still the land lay obdurately barren. At last, the only solution was for Zeus himself to speak to his brother Hades and command him to return Kore to her mother.

Kore, meanwhile, imprisoned in Hades' subterranean kingdom, had been exploring and had come upon a tree bearing strange fruit. The hard, outer skin was a yellow colour, and when she broke the fruit open clusters of seeds were revealed, surrounded by juicy, red flesh. Kore put the fruit to her lips and sucked in some of the flesh. It tasted bitter-sweet, not to her liking, and she threw the rest away. But in that one mouthful, she had swallowed four of the seeds, and they had sealed her fate. The fruit was the pomegranate, the 'apple of many seeds', the magical fruit of sexual union. Swallowing even part of it bound Kore to Hades in the sacred ties of marriage. She was now his wife, and had a new name: she was Persephone, Queen of the Underworld.

Knowing that she was bound to him, Hades consented to release the daughter of Demeter – but only for part of the year. For four months, one for every seed swallowed, she must stay with him in his dark realm. Demeter, reluctantly, agreed to this compromise. But for those four months every year, she goes into mourning for her daughter, neglecting the land so that it sleeps and lies barren, waiting for Kore's return when it will burst into fresh growth once more.

That is how winter came into the world, and so it has continued, from that day to this.

EROS AND PSYCHE

Long, long ago, there lived a king who had three daughters who were famed far and wide for their beauty, but the youngest was the most beautiful of all. Her name was Psyche, which means Soul, and her face was as fair as a spring morning. Indeed, so fair was she that she roused the jealousy of Aphrodite, goddess of love and beauty. In a fit of spite, the goddess sent her son Eros, the winged god of love, to wound the girl with one of his arrows. The arrows of Eros are the darts of love that pierce the heart and inspire in it passionate love for another. Aphrodite's plan was that, struck by her son's arrow, the hapless Psyche would fall in love with the very next knave or beggar who happened by.

Perhaps on this occasion the Fates were on Psyche's side, for the love-goddess's stratagem did not produce the desired results. The very moment Eros laid eyes on Psyche, he was so overcome by her beauty that he wounded himself with the arrow he had intended for her, and thus it was he, not she, who fell hopelessly and irrevocably in love with the other.

Psyche, of course, was blissfully unaware of the drama going on around her, for the god of love had not made himself visible to her.

Meanwhile, in the palace of Psyche's father the king, everyone was in a flurry of activity, for the wedding of her eldest sister was shortly to be celebrated. Hardly had they packed away the plates of gold and the jewel-encrusted goblets than they had to get them out again for the marriage of Psyche's second sister.

But for the beautiful Psyche herself there were no suitors. Her father wondered greatly at this and suspected the hand of the gods in the affair – particularly that of Aphrodite,

MAGICAL FRUIT

IN THE GARDEN of Paradise a magic tree grows, and on it hangs golden fruit. It is the fruit exchanged between Aphrodite and Paris; it is the fruit that grows in the orchards of Avalon; it is the fruit that grows across the sea from Ireland in Emain Ablach; it is the fruit that grows in the Garden of the Hesperides that blooms on a paradise island beyond the setting sun. The fruit, quite simply, is the apple.

In Greek myth, as in the mythologies and folklore of other European traditions, the apple has special status as a fruit of magic potency. When Paris was called upon to judge the beauty contest between Aphrodite, Hera, and Athene, the winner's prize was to be the golden Apple of Discord. Aphrodite's bribe that Paris would have the 'most beautiful woman in the world' – Helen of Troy – swayed his judgment and he conferred the apple on her. Here, the apple is a fruit of fate, for it sets in motion the bloody, ten-year-long Trojan War.

The apples in the Garden of the Hesperides were fruits of eternal life. They had been given as a wedding gift to Hera by Gaia, Mother Earth, who had sent the magic tree in its entirety to her granddaughter on her marriage to Zeus. The association of a Tree of Life, which contains in its fruit the concentrated essence of existence, with Hera is wholly appropriate, for as a mother-goddess type she is the source of being. The image is further strengthened by the identity of the giver of the gift – Gaia, the Earth, in which all living things have their origin.

Hera plants her Tree of Life in the garden of paradise which, like all such havens, lies on an island in the far west. Here it is watched over by the serpent Ladon and nymphs known as the Hesperides, after Hesperos, the evening star. In ancient paintings, the Hesperides are depicted watering the Tree from urns containing the Water of Life. The Apples of Eternal Youth, the Tree of Life, the Water of Life, the Serpent of Regeneration, the Garden of Paradise, the Island of the Blessed beyond the sunset – these combined images occur repeatedly in mythologies from as far apart as Sumeria in the east through Greece to Ireland in the far west.

Another, related magic fruit that occurs in Greek mythology is the pomegranate, the 'apple of many seeds'. In one legend, it was a pomegranate tree that sprang from the spilt blood of the murdered child Dionysos. More famously, it was the fruit that Hades cunningly contrived for Persephone to eat. Its seeds, thus planted in her body, forced her to remain in his underground kingdom for one third of every year; when liberated from this contract and allowed to return to the world again, it – and she – was 'reborn'.

whom he knew could display a jealous nature. And so he went to consult an oracle to discover what he should do. To his great dismay, for he loved his youngest daughter most of all, the oracle instructed him to dress Psyche in her bridal robes and take her up to the top of a particular mountain where he should abandon her to her fate.

The king was desolated at these words but knew that it was the greatest foolishness to ignore an oracle, for it was not given to mortals to see what might come of a particular action, however unwise it seemed. And so, that very night, Psyche was dressed in the finest bridal gown and led in torchlit procession to the very top of the mountain in question, where her father bid her a tearful farewell and left her to whatever death he was sure awaited her.

Now the poor girl was quite alone in the world. All the torches that had lighted her way up had long since gone, and around her was nothing but impenetrable darkness. She shivered with fear and wept tears of sorrow. Was this how she was to end her life, all alone on a mountain top? Or would some monster of the night swoop down and carry her off to his lair to devour her?

Presently, as she sat there wondering what her fate might be, she felt a warm breeze caress her hair and play with the folds of her gown, and found herself lifted in the arms of Zephyrus, the West Wind. Zephyrus gently carried her up over the peaks and down into a green valley, where he deposited her on a bank of sweet violets. Soothed by their perfume and exhausted by the terrors and strangeness of her experience, she fell into a deep and unshakeable sleep.

When she awoke in the morning and looked around her, she was amazed to see before her a magnificent palace. A broad flight of steps led up to it, and its marble columns and walls were carved and painted and decorated in patterns of gold and lapis lazuli and other precious stones, and within its central courtyard a fountain played. Charmed by this magical apparition, Psyche entered the building and began to explore the rooms, each of which appeared more gorgeous that the last. But nowhere, in all of this magnificence, was there any sign of life, just faint, almost imperceptible murmurings as if invisible beings busied themselves in the empty spaces.

At last, Psyche came to a room where a clear fire burned and a delicious repast was laid. Hungry and tired by now, she sat down and ate her fill, and as she did so, dusk began to fall. Long, blue shadows inked their way across the floors and night, the domain of magic, claimed the world. The fire had burnt out now, and in the darkness that enveloped her Psyche felt the air stir and heard a rushing of invisible wings. The poor girl was terrified, but a soft voice whispered in her ear:

'Do not be afraid, for I will not harm you. You cannot imagine how much I love you, and all I wish is for you, if you can, to love me a little in return. If you stay here in this palace as my bride, you will want for nothing – only please say you will stay!'

The voice of the invisible speaker was so gentle, so loving, that Psyche's fears evaporated. Why should she not stay? What awaited her back in her father's home? Spinsterhood and the commiserations of her married sisters? At least in this beautiful place her every need would be catered for, and so she determined to remain. From now on, her life in the magical palace assumed a pattern as regular as the rising and setting of the sun. Every day was spent in the most pleasant pastimes imaginable and every night her mysterious lover would visit her. But not once did she see his face or his form, for he had warned her:

'Do not ever ask me to show myself to you, for if you see me I will have to leave you for ever.'

And Psyche was content with that.

The days passed and the months passed and in time Psyche began to miss her sisters and wished to see them again. It was therefore agreed that Zephyrus would bring them to the palace, as he had brought Psyche herself. But before the West Wind set off on his errand, Psyche's invisible lover gave her a solemn but cryptic warning:

'Pay no attention to what your sisters tell you, for if you do, all will end between you and me,' he said.

When the sisters arrived at the palace, they greeted Psyche with much affection and exclaimed in delight at everything they saw, but in truth they were jealous of her good fortune, and wished to find a chink in her happiness, to burrow away for a vulnerable spot in her apparently unassailable contentment. It did not take them long.

'Tell us, sister dear,' they said, 'do you not think it very strange that your lover has never shown you his face? What has he to hide? Have you ever considered that he might be a hideous, deformed creature who dares not show himself? Or perhaps – heaven forbid – he is an ogre waiting his moment to eat you up! Now please, be sensible. Take a lamp and look on his face while he sleeps. You must find out the truth, for your own safety.'

The seeds of doubt may take root in the most unlikely of soils, and after her sisters had returned home, Psyche pondered long and hard over what they had said, and the more she pondered the more fearful she became. Why had her lover never allowed himself to be seen? And why did he only ever visit her at night?

She determined to discover the answer, and that very night she took an oil lamp and crept over to where he was sleeping and held the lamp so that the light fell on his face … and the face she saw was quite the most exquisite she had ever laid eyes on, for she was looking on the face of Love itself.

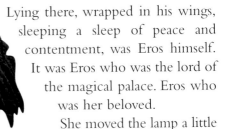

Lying there, wrapped in his wings, sleeping a sleep of peace and contentment, was Eros himself. It was Eros who was the lord of the magical palace. Eros who was her beloved.

She moved the lamp a little so that she might see him better, but in doing so let fall a drop of the burning-hot oil which landed on the god's shoulder, and he woke. He gazed at her for a moment with sad reproach in his eyes. And then, in a flash, he was gone, and so was everything else. The palace vanished. The fountain vanished. The green valley vanished. The bank of sweet violets vanished. And there was Psyche, back where she had been at the outset of her adventure, on top of the lonely mountain.

Now began the time of her real trials, as she wandered off into the wide, wide world to seek her beloved whom she had lost through her own gullibility and foolishness.

Far and farther, over hill and over dale, over mountain and over valley, Psyche journeyed in her quest until at last she arrived at the abode of Aphrodite, whom she knew to be the mother of her beloved. Not knowing that the goddess was the source of all her troubles, she appealed to her for help.

'There's a price for everything,' snapped the goddess. 'If you want me to lead you to my son, you must first prove yourself worthy by performing a little task I need done.'

She pointed to a large jumble of seeds lying nearby, the food of doves and sparrows, composed of wheat, barley, millet and other grains.

'Take these seeds and separate them into piles of their various kinds,' Aphrodite commanded, 'and get it finished by nightfall!'

The task was impossible. Psyche sat down, defeated, with her head in her hands, and wept.

But just then, a small black ant emerged from behind the pile of seeds, followed by a long line of others, and the ants all set to and, with the precision of well-drilled soldiers, made short work of dividing the seeds, wheat with wheat, barley with barley, millet with millet, and so on until all were sorted. By the time the sun had reddened the sky on his way to his rest, all the seeds lay in orderly piles.

When Aphrodite saw that the task was completed, and within the time limit she had set, she was extremely annoyed.

'This was not done by your own hand alone!' she said angrily, and the following morning she set Psyche an even harder task.

'Fetch me some of the fleece from those golden sheep,' she ordered, pointing to a flock grazing on the opposite bank of a river. Now these sheep were wild and dangerous beasts, with sharp horns and venomous bites. The task was impossible, and Psyche, defeated, sat down and wept.

But just then, she heard a reed by the side of river whispering to her.

'Wait,' it said, 'until the sun is low for then the sheeps' fierceness will be depleted, and you will easily be able to gather as much of their shed fleece as you wish.' And that is exactly what she did.

CINDERELLAS

THE CLASSICAL tale of the trials of Psyche and Eros, the god of erotic love, forms part of ancient literature for it was included in *The Golden Ass*, written by Lucius Apuleius in about AD 160. Its familiar story-motifs of the 'jealous mother' (Aphrodite), the 'prohibition' (Psyche must not look on Eros) and the 'impossible tasks' (sorting seeds) give it a powerful folk-tale feeling, although mythic elements are present in the personae of Eros and Aphrodite, and in the ascension of Psyche to Olympus.

The tale, in fact, belongs to the genre of Cinderella stories, of which there are more than 300 variations. All feature a heroine who is faced with a set of trials, which she accomplishes – often with supernatural or animal help – either in a domestic setting or in the wide world beyond. At the end of her trials, she is recognized for her true worth and achieves her reward and rightful status, according to the threefold structure of crisis–trial–resolution which typifies all Quests. Those familiar with *Beauty and the Beast* will instantly recognize Eros's magical palace with its semi-absent host, while the task of separating the seeds is identical to that in several versions of *Cinderella*. However, in its structure Psyche's story most closely resembles the lyrically beautiful *East of the Sun and West of the Moon*, the Norwegian wonder tale and its Scottish equivalent, *The Black Bull of Norroway*.

When Aphrodite saw that the task was completed, she was even more annoyed than before.

'This was not done by your own hand alone!' she said angrily, and the following morning she set Psyche an even harder task.

'Take this crystal vase and fill it from the Spring of Forgetfulness,' she commanded.

Now the water of this fateful fountain was as freezing as ice, and it lay at the top of a rocky mountain, guarded by two dragons that lived in caves and that never slept. When Psyche arrived at this place, she was dumbstruck with terror. The spring was higher than anyone could possibly climb, and no one could hope to escape the dragons.

The task was impossible, and Psyche sat down and gave herself up for lost.

But just then, an eagle swooped down, bore off the vase, filled it at the spring, and returned it to Psyche.

When Aphrodite saw that the task was completed, she was furious.

'This was not done by your own hand alone!' she said angrily, and the following morning she set Psyche the hardest task of all.

'Take this box,' she declared, handing her a small casket, 'and go down to the underworld, to Persephone Queen of the Dead, and ask her to fill the box with some of her beauty.'

This, Psyche felt sure, would be the undoing of her, for none can travel to the land of the dead and return. She might just as well end it now, for without her beloved, life was not worth living. So she climbed to the top of a tall tower, intending to throw herself off. But just as she was teetering on the edge, looking down at the vast drop below her, she heard the stones of the tower crying out to her.

'Wait, wait!' they called. 'Do you not know that there is a path that leads to the underworld? Follow it and take with you two coins for Charon the Boatman and two pieces of bread for Cerberus who guards the gate.'

And that is exactly what she did, although the task filled her with fear and loathing for it was the hardest she had ever been required to do.

Passing along the dark road to the underworld, she came at last to the Styx, the River of Hate that flows nine times around the Elysian Fields, where live the dead. There she gave the first coin to Charon to ferry her across the river. On the other bank stood Cerberus, the three-headed watchdog of hell, and she offered the first piece of bread to Cerberus, to placate the hound so that he would let her by.

At last, she arrived in the presence of Persephone, she handed her the pyxis, the casket, and the Queen of the Dead generously filled it with some of her beauty and sealed it.

Psyche returned by the same way as she had come, giving the second piece of bread to Cerberus and the second coin to Charon. Her arduous quest over, she now turned her attentions to the casket. Aphrodite had beauty a-plenty. Surely she would not notice if Psyche helped herself to a little – just the merest speck – of the contents of the box? It was the least she deserved, after all she had been through. Gently, she raised the lid and peered inside. The casket appeared to be empty, but in opening it Psyche had released the potent but invisible vapours condensed within it. As they rose, she breathed them in and fell into a deep swoon, the twin of death.

There she might be lying still had not Eros, now recovered from the wound caused by the burning oil, seen her sad plight and begged Zeus, the Master of Heaven, to take pity on her. Even Aphrodite relented, for Psyche had – albeit with help – completed every task set her, and her trials were over.

So it was that Hermes, messenger of the gods, was despatched to bring Psyche to Olympus. And when the Master of Heaven himself put to her lips the cup containing the elixir of life, and she drank the honeyed nectar, two wings like those of a butterfly sprouted from her shoulders and she became one with the immortals.

And then there was such a wedding! The god called Love was married to the girl named Soul, and if all the merrymaking and rejoicing have not ceased, well … then they continue still.

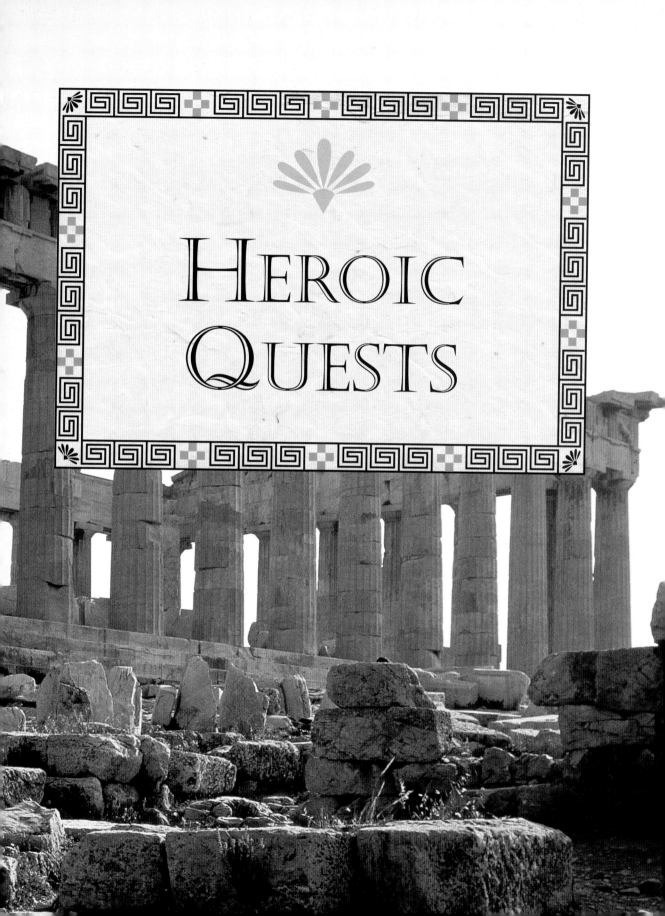

HEROIC
QUESTS

PERSEUS AND THE GORGON

THIS IS A TALE OF THE inevitability of fate, of a grandfather who sought to escape his destiny and a grandson who trusted to fortune, and how the one caused the downfall of the other.

The grandfather's name was Acrisius, and he was king of Argos. Acrisius had an only daughter by the name of Danaë, and he had learned from the oracle at Delphi that the son born to her would, when grown, be the means of his death. There was an easy enough solution to this problem, he thought – he would simply keep Danaë incarcerated so that it was impossible for her to come into contact with men. So he ordered a subterranean chamber built – or, some say, a bronze tower – in which he imprisoned his daughter. In this best-laid plan, however, Acrisius had overlooked one factor: Zeus.

When Zeus was looking down one day from his pinnacle on lofty Olympus to see what he might see, he spied the lovely Danaë weeping all alone in her tomb, and decided to pay her a visit. Neither stone nor bronze were any barrier to Zeus. In an instant, he had transformed himself into a shower of gold and seeped through the solid walls of her prison, into her chamber, and into her body, and in no time at all Danaë had conceived a child by him, a boy dusted with the gold of the sun, who would be called Perseus.

When Acrisius discovered that, despite all his best efforts, his daughter had given birth to a boy, he was panic-stricken. Flesh of his flesh she might be, but saving his own skin mattered more, so he decided to banish Danaë and her infant to a place from which the boy might never return to do him harm. Hardening his heart to her piteous pleas, Acrisius set his own daughter and her child adrift on the sea, there to meet whatever fortune awaited them.

What lay in store for them, however, was quite other than the king's imaginings, for the chest with its precious cargo did not sink to the bottom of the sea, but bobbed along on a benign current, until at last it washed up on the shores of the island of Seriphos, where it was caught in the nets of Dictys, brother to Polydectes who was king of the island. Dictys took the bedraggled pair in, gave them food and shelter, and welcomed them into his home.

Time passed, and in the passing of time, Perseus grew into a strong and brave young man. But it was not Perseus on whom the king, Polydectes, was focusing his attentions. It was his mother, beautiful Danaë, whose image filled the king's waking moments, and whom he wished to claim for his own. But first he must rid himself of the son, who might stand in his way. The king therefore conceived a cruel plan that would send the young man on a long and perilous journey. He announced to the world that he wished to marry a princess by the name of Hippodameia, and declared that gold, silver, jewels, furs, horses, chariots, slaves, and all manner of other treasures would be graciously received as wedding gifts.

Perseus had no riches or possessions to offer but, not wishing to be outdone, he could think of only one gift that would outshine all the others.

'I will bring you the head of Medusa!' he declared.

The silence that fell at these words stifled all laughter and chatter among those present. Everyone had heard tell of the abhorrent Gorgons, the three winged sisters whose names were Stheno, Euryale, and Medusa. Instead of hands of flesh they had hands of bronze, instead of teeth they had boar tusks, instead of locks of hair they had tangles of writhing serpents, and their gaze was so cold that it turned people to stone. No one had ever faced the Gorgons and lived … and this, of course, was exactly the kind of daredevil exploit Polydectes had hoped Perseus would suggest, an exploit from which, the king was sure, the young man would never return.

Despite the entreaties of his mother, Perseus was determined on his quest, and made preparations to leave the very next day.

A journey of a thousand miles, says the sage, begins with the first step, and so it was that Perseus stepped out into the wide, wide world on the greatest quest he would ever undertake – without the faintest idea of which way to go. All he knew was that the Gorgons were rumoured to live on a barren island at the very ends of the earth. But help often comes in unbidden ways, and as Perseus was standing on the shore deliberating, the goddess Athene and the winged god Hermes suddenly appeared before him.

'Leave off thy sighing and vexation,' said Athene, 'for I have come to aid thee. If thou wouldst know where the three Gorgons live, thou must seek their sisters, the three Graeae.'

Then she gave Perseus her bronze shield and Hermes gave him his sickle, the only blade that would cut through the Gorgon's scales, and offered to accompany Perseus part of the way.

Perseus and Hermes travelled northward, to the land of dusk that lay in the mists of the sea, where lived the Graeae, the Grey Sisters – Enyo the Warlike, Pemphredo the Wasp, and Deino the Terror. When they finally reached their destination, what they heard, drifting out of the denseness of the fog, were three bickering, querulous voices.

'Sister, it is my turn. Givest thou it to me!'

'Nay, sister, I beg to differ. I assure thee it is mine!'

'Sister dearest, thou art mistaken. It is mine!'

The voices belonged to the Graeae and they were arguing over the single eye and the single tooth which were all that remained to them on account of their great age, and which they would pass from one to the other as need demanded.

'Good day to you, grandmother' said Perseus, seizing his opportunity and deftly snatching the eye as it passed from one hand to the next, '… and good day to you,' as he snatched the tooth. 'Dear ladies, you must excuse my impertinence, but I am in need of information. If you wish to see and to eat again, you must tell me where the Gorgons live.'

There was much muttering and grumbling and tutting and grinding of toothless gums, but at last the Graeae replied.

'If thou wouldst know where the three Gorgons live,' they croaked in unison, 'thou must seek the three Hesperides.'

The sweet-singing Hesperides were the Daughters of Night who guarded the golden apples of immortality in a garden on an island that lay beyond the setting sun.

Before leaving the Graeae, Perseus also elicited from them the whereabouts of the Stygian Nymphs, who possessed three magical objects that he needed for his errand: a pair of winged sandals so that he might fly as fast as Hermes; a helmet belonging to Hades, god of the underworld, that rendered the wearer invisible; and a magic pouch in which to place the Gorgon's head. Having acquired these treasures, and equipped also with the shield of Athene and the sickle of Hermes, Perseus set off alone to the far west, where the Hesperides lived. It was near the Hesperides that he would find the three serpent-haired sisters whom he sought.

At last he saw it, the dwelling place of the Gorgons. Hovering over it like some giant bird, Perseus noticed that this desolate spot was littered with rocks of all shapes and sizes. Some were tall, some were short, some were rounded and smooth, some were angular, jagged and thin; these rocks, he realized, were all the people petrified by the stony stare of the Gorgons – and there, in their midst, were the three sisters themselves, fast asleep, their tangled serpent locks wriggling and writhing over their faces.

Now of the three Gorgons, the only one who was mortal, the only one who could be killed, was Medusa. Taking care not to look in her face lest she wake and catch his eye, Perseus held up Athene's shield so that he could see Medusa's reflection in it, and then, his eye guided by this mirror image and his hand guided by Athene, he raised the sickle of Hermes and sliced through the Gorgon's neck with a single, swooping movement.

What chaos broke out then. A fountain of blood spouted from Medusa's neck and out of the foaming red tide rode a winged horse, Pegasus by name, and the warrior Chrysaor 'of the golden sword'. Stheno and Euryale, woken by the commotion, looked about wildly to discover their sister's assailant; and Perseus grabbed Medusa's head, stuffed it in the magic pouch, and made off with the Gorgons in vain pursuit, for Perseus was still protected by the helmet of invisibility.

Having escaped his pursuers and returning from his quest, Perseus stopped off in Ethiopia on his way back to Seriphos, and it was here that he came upon Andromeda, who had been chained to a rock as a sacrifice to a sea monster and was waiting, a helpless victim, to be devoured. Perseus fell in love with her at first sight, slew the approaching monster, cut through Andromeda's chains, and took her home with him as his wife.

When he arrived back at the palace of Polydectes, Danaë was overjoyed to see him again for she had thought he was lost for ever, and she told him that in his absence she had been cruelly used by the king. He approached the throne of Polydectes.

'Perseus!' said the king, suppressing his amazement. 'What a surprise … a pleasure … I never expected … I always hoped … how good to have you home!'

'The pleasure is mine,' said Perseus. 'And look, I have brought you your wedding gift,' and he pulled the head of Medusa out of the magic pouch and held it up before the king, who could not help but return its unblinking stare, and was instantly turned to stone.

Perseus then gave the head to Athene, who placed it on her shield, and he, Danaë and Andromeda left Seriphos and sailed for Argos, where Acrisius his grandfather still lived. When Acrisius, who thought he had rid himself of his grandson for good, heard that Perseus was alive and – worse still – was headed for Argos, he fled to the city of Larissa in Thessaly, so that he would not be in Argos when his grandson arrived.

Fortunately or unfortunately, the ship bearing Perseus and his companions just so happened to be blown off course to this same Larissa, where the people were holding celebratory games. Among the spectators was King Acrisius.

Fortunately or unfortunately, Perseus, a skilled athlete, was invited to join in the sport. Holding a discus in his hand, he began the wide curve of the throw.

Fortunately or unfortunately, as the discus left his hand and soared through the air in a mighty arc and was winging its way downward, a freak gust just so happened to blow it toward the crowd of spectators where, unerringly, it met its mark, striking Acrisius full on the forehead and killing him instantly.

Sadly, Perseus buried his grandfather, whose demise he had unwittingly caused. And so it was that all the schemes of Acrisius came to nothing in the end, for Death which he thought to escape in Argos had been waiting for him all along in Larissa.

THE LABOURS OF HERACLES

Looking down from his pinnacle on lofty Olympus to see what he might see, Zeus – Master of Heaven and cosmic philanderer – spotted something down in the palace of Thebes, down on the fertile plain of Boeotia, that caught his roving eye. That something was Alcmene, wife of Amphitryon. The sight of her inspired a passion in him, and it was in satisfying this passing passion that Zeus would father one of the greatest of all the great heroes of ancient Greece. This is how it all began.

Amphitryon, grandson of the mighty Gorgon-slaying Perseus, was king of Thebes. Now it so happened one day that the king was called away to war, and had to leave his wife Alcmene, also a grandchild of Perseus, alone in the palace. It was at this very moment that Zeus glanced down from his mountain eyrie in the direction of Thebes, and saw her. The scene was irrestible to him – a beautiful young queen all on her own with no one to share her bed. He decided to pay her a visit.

On this occasion Zeus chose a particularly subtle deceit. Stealing down to earth, he assumed the likeness of the absent king, Amphitryon – a likeness exact in every detail down to the very last hair on his chin. Delighted to see her husband home again so early, Alcmene lay with him. When the real king, returned from battle, arrived in her bedroom a day or two later, the queen was pleasantly surprised to find her husband's ardour still as strong as it had been only a few nights before, and from this double union came a double conception. Alcmene became pregnant with twins.

On the day that the queen was due to give birth, Zeus – proud prospective father that he was – swore an oath up in Olympus: the descendant of Perseus that was about to be born would one day rule all of Greece! When Hera, his long-suffering wife, heard her husband's pronouncement, she decided to intervene. She went at once to Thebes, and by means of her divine power prolonged the labour of Alcmene so that another boy child was delivered first. This baby was Eurystheus and because this infant, too, was a descendant of Perseus, Zeus was forced to recognize him as the future king.

Alcmene, meanwhile, was finally delivered of her children. One was Iphicles, a gurgling infant like every other. However, his twin was altogether different, for destiny had chosen for him the hero's path, and his name would be renowned throughout the ancient world and would ring through all the centuries to come. Iphicles' twin was Heracles, strong man, braveheart and champion of Greece.

Even as an infant, Heracles was not like other children, and showed signs of precociousness early on. One night, when all the palace was fast asleep, two snakes – undoubtedly sent by Hera – came slithering across the nursery floor, intent on killing him. But while Iphicles, who was alongside his brother, screamed in terror, the baby Heracles showed no fear but simply picked the serpents up by their necks – one in each pink, plump, dimpled hand – and squeezed and squeezed until they were dead.

As Heracles grew up, he was taught all the things that noble Greek youths should know: how to play the lyre, how to reason and argue, how to drive a chariot, how to shoot arrows from a bow. He also spent some time living among herdsmen in the mountains, and it was here, leading this rugged life, that he developed his extraordinary physical strength and heavily muscled body.

There were other diversions, too. At the age of eighteen, while lying in wait for a ferocious lion that had been attacking Amphitryon's herds, Heracles took up brief residence in the house of King Thespius. Now this king happened to have fifty beautiful young daughters and Heracles, temporarily unoccupied, whiled away the empty hours by lying with all fifty maidens in a single night, a feat of which even Zeus would have been proud.

The beaming approval of his divine father was not, however, enough to protect our hero from the wrath of Hera. Throughout his growing years she had been keeping an eye on him, and she decided it was now time to interfere in his life again. By this time, Heracles had married Megara but their marriage, sadly, was not a happy one, and Hera was quick to seize her opportunity. The agent she chose to implement her plan was Lyssa, the Fury of Madness, one of the vengeful spirit sisters born of the blood of the castrated Ouranos. Day after day, night after night, Lyssa was with Heracles, never leaving his side, whispering dark thoughts in his ear, sowing the seeds of madness in his mind, until in the end he lost all reason and fell on his own wife and children and murdered them.

When he came to his senses and saw what he had done, Heracles was overcome with shame and horror, and went to Delphi to consult the oracle there as to what he should do to expiate the hideous crime he had committed. The oracle told him that he must place himself in the service of none other than King Eurystheus. Oh, how Hera must have gloated! This Eurystheus was the very one who, with Hera's contrivance, had usurped Heracles of the kingship ordained for him by Zeus.

And this is when Heracles' real trials began, for it would be many a year before the stain of his sin was removed.

In the palace at Mycenæ, Heracles stood before the throne of Eurytheus and offered himself in service to the king, as the oracle had decreed. An act of humility such as this was not easy for a man as brave and strong as he.

The king looked Heracles over. The newcomer had all the appearance of a god. Taut muscles rippled under the golden sheen of his skin, his shoulders were broad, his torso lean and trim, his eye fine and clear, and coils of luxuriant, glossy hair tumbled down his forehead and curled around his ears. It was not without a pang of jealousy that the king also noticed the flutter that Heracles' arrival was causing among the ladies of the court. He felt a rising tide of irritation.

'So this Heracles …' the king brooded, '… this Heracles who would have stolen my right to be king has come to place himself in my service, has he? Well, we'll see how swaggering and brave he is when I've finished with him.'

Eurystheus thought of all the dangerous errands he could send him on, the ones that no one else would dare to tackle, in the remotest regions, the furthest outposts of the kingdom and beyond and – oh, the joy of it – because of the conditions of his employ, Heracles would not be able to refuse any of the king's commands. In short, Eurystheus decided that the time his rival would spend in his service would be far from pleasant. He began to plot Heracles' first terrifying labour.

THE LION OF NEMEA

'Over in Nemea …' Eurystheus began, 'there's a lion that's causing a little spot of bother. Be a good fellow and kill it for me. Oh, and by the way, bring me the skin as a trophy.'

To remove the stain of his sin, Heracles had no choice but to obey. The lion of Nemea was a ferocious beast that had been killing sheep and cattle all around and had even taken a child or two. No one in the region felt safe.

When Heracles first came upon the beast, he aimed his arrows at it but they just seemed to glance off the animal's pelt. Weapons were clearly useless; he would have to use his bare hands. Summoning up all his prodigious strength, Hercules fell on the lion. Hair flew and fur flew and blood flew in such a whirl that you could not tell who was man and who

was beast, but in the end the lion lay dead at Heracles' feet. Incredibly, he had strangled it, just as he had strangled the two snakes when he was a baby.

When Heracles presented himself before Eurystheus, with a magnificent lion's skin casually draped across his shoulder, the king was not pleased to see him.

He began to plot Heracles' second dangerous labour.

THE HYDRA OF LERNA

'I hear you killed two snakes as a baby,' the king began. 'Well, now that you're grown, you'll be able to take on something bigger – the Hydra of Lerna. It has nine heads, so I'm told, but I'm sure you'll be able to despatch the monster in no time.'

To remove the stain of his sin, Heracles had no choice but to obey. The Hydra did indeed have nine heads and poisonous breath as well. It lived in the marshes, where it ravaged both crops and herds and killed anyone who came near it with its poisonous breath.

In the company of his nephew Iolaus, Heracles set off for Lerna. There he enticed the monster out of its lair by means of flaming arrows, and attempted to strike off its heads with his powerful club. But for every head that rolled, two new ones grew. The serpent seemed invincible, until Iolaus suggested that they set a neighbouring forest alight and, with blazing brands taken from the fire, burned the heads instead.

The plan worked perfectly, and when all but the last head was gone, Heracles cut off that one, too, and buried it. Then he dipped his arrows in the Hydra's poisonous blood to make them even more deadly.

When Heracles presented himself before Eurystheus again, not only unharmed but also carrying a quiverful of lethal arrows, the king was not pleased to see him.

He began to plan Heracles' third hazardous labour.

THE BOAR OF ERYMANTHUS

'Over on Mount Erymanthus, so they tell me, a wild boar is causing trouble,' the king began. 'Well, I told them, I know just the man to deal with it – you! But this time, please, no animal skins or poisoned arrows. I want the beast brought back alive.'

To remove the stain of his sin, Heracles had no choice but to obey. By ordering him to capture the boar and lead it all the way back to Mycenae, rather than kill it, Eurystheus hoped that this would give the enraged animal plenty of time to gore Heracles to death.

Heracles set off but on his way to the mountain was temporarily delayed by a horde of troublesome centaurs, who were half-man and half-horse, and on whom he was forced to use some of his poisoned arrows. At last, however, he reached his destination and sighted his quarry – a massive, hairy, grunting boar with enormous, razor-sharp tusks. Now in some situations, the element of surprise is worth a thousand weapons, and so it was that, as the beast pawed the ground, making ready to charge, Heracles swiftly stooped down, lifted the startled animal up, and slung it over his broad shoulders where it seemed content to stay.

When Heracles presented himself before Eurystheus again, with a snuffling, snorting wild boar draped around his shoulders as if it were no more than a purring kitten, the king was terrified and took refuge in a large urn, where he seethed in muffled secret.

He began to plot Heracles' fourth hazardous labour.

THE BIRDS OF STYMPHALUS

'Over on the marshes of Stymphalus,' the king began, 'the people cannot graze their sheep and cattle for fear of attack by birds. I've never heard such nonsense myself, but the people continue to complain, so go over there, my good man, and calm the situation down.'

To remove the stain of his sin, Heracles had no choice but to obey. Of course, as the king knew only too well, the Birds of Stymphalus were no innocent creatures but winged monsters with beaks and claws of iron. Their feathers had tips as sharp as nails, and in flight they would drop these like a shower of knives to lacerate and slice the flesh of any living thing below. As to their number, they were so many that when they arose from the marshes in a great whirring, clattering cloud, they blotted out the sun.

For this labour, Heracles decided on a simple tactic. Instead of trying to kill the birds – a near impossibility because of their numbers – he would scare them away. So he called them out by banging with his lance on his shield, held over his head for protection, and ringing a large bell. The shattering din alerted the birds who were, like all others of their kind, afraid of loud noises. They rose in vast billows from the marshes, scattering their feathers as they went, and flew away. Heracles despatched the few that remained with his poisoned arrows.

When Heracles presented himself before Eurystheus again, alive and well and with barely a hair out of place, the king was not pleased to see him. In fact, he did not feel inclined to give him a welcome at all.

He began to devise Heracles' fifth arduous labour.

THE HIND OF CERYNEIA

'I have heard tell,' the king mused, 'of a wonderful hind that roams the forests of Mount Ceryneia. Her horns are of gold, her hooves of bronze, and so fleet of foot is she that none has yet been able to catch her. I have a fancy to see her. Bring her to me!'

To remove the stain of his sin, Heracles had no choice but to obey. Gleefully, Eurystheus pictured what would happen. The strong man would run and run, the sweat pouring from his body, yet all in vain for no matter how fast he ran, or for how long, the hind would always be just out of reach. With any luck, Heracles would collapse from exhaustion and die, for even he, strong though he was, must have his limits. There was added danger, too, in that the hind was rumoured to be under the protection of Artemis, goddess of hunting, who would not look favourably on one pursuing her pet. Oh yes, Eurystheus could see it all now. It was such visions that kept the king warm at night.

The picture in the king's mind was not very different from what really happened. Heracles came upon the beautiful hind in the forest, and the chase began. The hero was fast but the hind was faster, and she led him over hill and down dale, up mountains and through rivers, and into far-distant lands he had never known. But instead of collapsing from exhaustion, Heracles just kept on running and running until a whole year had gone by and the chase had, like all the best adventures, come full circle back to where it began.

There stood the hind, unable to run any longer, and Heracles would have laid his hands on her there and then had he not looked up and seen, in the light of the full moon, a shining figure. It was Artemis herself. She forbade him to touch the hind for the animal belonged to her, but told him to report to Eurystheus all that had happened, and to consider his fifth labour done.

When Heracles presented himself before Eurystheus again, cool and refreshed after a whole year running around the world, and gave him Artemis' message, the king was not pleased. Wild beasts, wild birds, the wrath of a goddess – was there nothing that the strong man could not overcome?

He began to dream up Heracles' sixth hideous labour.

THE STABLES OF AUGEAS

'A king's lot is a wearisome one, is it not?' Eurystheus began pensively. 'As if ruling a kingdom and fighting wars were not sufficient to keep one occupied, one then has the servant problem. Why, poor King Augeas cannot persuade any of his stablehands to remain because of the state of his stables. They are filthy! The dung has been piling up for years, and entertaining royal guests is impossible because of the stench. I told him you would clean out the stables for him.'

To remove the stain of his sin, Heracles had no choice but to obey. The thought of the strong man knee-deep in stinking cattle dung, getting it under his nails and in his skin and, with any luck, in his hair, too, gave Eurystheus many an idle moment's amusement.

But the king had not allowed for Heracles' inventiveness. Without further ado, the hero made a breach in the stable wall and diverted the course of two rivers, the Alpheus and the Peneius, so that they gushed through the stables like a giant jet of water and sluiced out the accumulated ordure of decades.

When Heracles presented himself before Eurystheus again, fresh and sweet-smelling as a spring morning, the king was not pleased to see him. Even the most humble tasks were not beneath him, it seemed, and he carried them out with equanimity and efficiency.

He began to devise Heracles' seventh life-threatening labour.

THE BULL OF CRETE

'I want you to go to Crete,' said the king. 'The country is being terrorized by a mad bull. Be a good fellow and kill the animal, would you?'

To remove the stain of his sin, Heracles had no choice but to obey. Now this ferocious beast was, of course, none other than the white bull from the sea sent by the god Poseidon to Minos, to prove the latter's rightful status as king of Crete. When Minos refused to sacrifice the animal in return, as promised, Poseidon inflicted a terrible punishment. First he made the king's wife fall in love with the bull, and then he drove the bull mad. Having coupled with the queen, the crazed animal was then free to roam the island, terrifying all he met.

Heracles was undeterred. Having already faced so many terrors, what was a wild bull to one such as he? He easily captured the animal and, hoisting it onto his back, returned to Mycenae.

When Heracles presented himself before Eurystheus again, alive and well and with a white bull in tow that seemed as docile as a spring lamb, the king was not pleased to see him, and the welcome he gave was from clenched lips.

He began plotting Heracles' eighth terrifying labour.

THE MARES OF DIOMEDES

'I need some fresh blood for my stables,' the king announced, 'and I hear that King Diomedes has just the quality of mares I need to breed from. Ask him if he will agree.'

To remove the stain of his sin, Heracles had no choice but to obey. Of course, the king's apparently straightforward command concealed dark intentions, for these mares, as Eurystheus well knew, were no ordinary horses, but creatures who fed on human flesh. Heracles, he hoped, would provide their next meal.

Heracles embarked on his mission with a group of others and eventually captured the mares. The men of Diomedes descended on the thieves and a ferocious battle ensued. The victor, as in all previous labours, was Heracles, and he fed the wicked Diomedes to his own horses.

This was not Heracles' only triumph on this occasion, for before he returned to the king's palace, he successfully fought Thanatos – Death – himself, for the life of Queen Alcestis of Pherae.

When Heracles presented himself before Eurystheus again, positively glowing with health and with not a single lump of flesh missing, the king was not pleased to see him. Seven labours set, seven labours accomplished. There must be something – or someone – who could get the better of the strong man.

He began to plan Heracles' ninth spine-chilling labour.

THE GIRDLE OF HIPPOLYTE

'You know how it is with young women,' whispered the king, conspiratorially, 'they love fine clothes and jewels. Well, my daughter Admete has conceived a great yearning for the Girdle of Hippolyte. She says she will positively die if she does not have it. Fetch the girdle for her!'

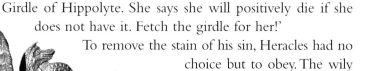

To remove the stain of his sin, Heracles had no choice but to obey. The wily king, of course, was fully aware of where he was sending his messenger, for Hippolyte was queen of the Amazons, fierce warrior-women, and her richly adorned girdle had been given to her personally by Ares, god of war, as a mark of her sovereignty. Eurystheus did not imagine for a moment that she would agree to part with it.

After a long time or a short time, Heracles reached the country where Hippolyte and her Amazons lived. He put his request to the queen who, at first, seemed prepared to hand over her girdle as a gift to the princess. Hera, however, up on lofty Olympus, had been keeping a watchful eye on the affairs of Heracles and decided that it was time to sow a little discord. So she spread a rumour that Heracles had secretly come to abduct Hippolyte, whereupon the Amazons, like soldier ants defending their queen, seized their weapons and made ready to attack. Heracles, in turn, believing that they had intended to capture him all along, retaliated and slaughtered them all, including the queen. Such was the sorry outcome of this particular quest.

When Heracles presented himself before Eurystheus again, with the dazzling girdle in his hand, the king was not pleased to see him. Since Heracles had been in action, there were hardly any monsters or nameless terrors left to confront … but Eurystheus would think of one, even if it meant sending Heracles to the ends of the earth.

He began to plan Heracles' tenth impossible labour.

THE CATTLE OF GERYON

'When you were younger, so I'm told, you lived amongst herdsmen,' the king said. 'Well, I have just the job for a man who has a way with cattle. Bring me the red cattle of Geryon.'

To remove the stain of his sin, Heracles had no choice but to obey. The task sounded straightforward enough, but Geryon was in fact a fearsome giant, with three bodies and three heads, six legs and six arms, and a pair of wings for good measure. He had an enormous herd of red cattle which every evening, as the sun was setting, he would drive into a dark cave. Furthermore, he lived as far as it is possible to go, at the very ends of the earth on an island that lay beyond the setting sun.

To reach this outlandish spot, Heracles borrowed the golden cup of the sun god Helios, in which the god would sail every night, from west to east, after he had slipped behind the horizon. As well as being singularly well-suited to this particular journey, the cup had the additional advantage of being able to enlarge or decrease in size, depending on the needs of the person using it.

As soon as he reached the giant's island, Heracles set to work. First he killed Geryon's guard-dog, then his herdsman, and then he saw Geryon himself, with his flailing arms and swinging clubs, roaring and shouting from his three throats at once. But victory comes to those who act fast, and without delaying an instant, Heracles lifted his bow, let fly his poisoned arrows, and the giant fell dead on the spot.

Heracles herded all the cattle into the sun-cup of Helios, which obligingly swelled to accommodate them, and set off on the return journey, which was beset with difficulties. The sons of Poseidon, the sea god, tried to steal the cattle; Hera contrived to stampede them by tormenting them with her favourite weapon, a gadfly; and in Gaul, where he stopped for a while, Heracles found time to put an end to the practice of human sacrifice. It was a busy time for our hero.

When, at last, Heracles presented himself before Eurystheus again, alive and well and with a huge herd of cattle trotting along meekly behind him, Eurystheus was not pleased to see him. Ten labours accomplished, ten victories to boast about, and Heracles was still standing. Eurystheus was beginning to lose patience. If he had sent him to the ends of the earth once, he would send him there again, and perhaps this time it would work.

He began to plan Heracles' eleventh incredible labour.

THE APPLES OF THE HESPERIDES

'Far away in a paradise garden,' said the king, 'grows a tree that bears magical apples. I wish to taste them. Fetch them for me.'

To remove the stain of his sin, Heracles had no choice but to obey. The fruits of which Eurystheus spoke were the famed golden apples of eternal life belonging to the goddess Hera herself. They grew on an orchard island to the far, far west, beyond the sunset, where they were tended by three sisters called the Hesperides, and guarded by a dragon whose name was Ladon.

Everyone had heard of this wonderful garden, but no one could tell Heracles exactly how to get there, so he set off to find it by himself, going in a north-westerly direction. But his fame and reputation preceded him, attracting adversaries at every turn like moths to a flame, each eager to see if he, and no other, could be the one to overcome the great hero.

By the River Rhone, nymphs told Heracles to ask the way of Nereus, the Old Man of the Sea. After capturing him, Heracles refused to let him go even though the god tried to frighten him with a display of shape-shifting. At last, perceiving that the strong man was unimpressed, Nereus resumed his normal shape and told Heracles to go southward.

In the Caucasus, Heracles stopped to free Prometheus whose liver was being devoured by an eagle, in punishment for stealing fire from heaven. In Egypt, he escaped being offered as a human sacrifice. In Libya, he fought a terrible giant, son of Gaia, who drew new strength every time his foot touched the ground; Heracles defeated him by holding him up in the air. Stopping to rest after his struggle with the giant, Heracles was attacked in his sleep by Pygmies, but he sewed them up into his lion skin. At last, close to his destination, he saw the man he had been looking for – Atlas, the Titan whose job it was to stand for all eternity holding up the sky.

Knowing that Atlas would do anything for a rest, Heracles offered to take the weight off his shoulders for a while if he, in return, would bring him three of the magical golden apples. He further eased the Titan's task by killing the serpent Ladon, who guarded the precious fruit, with one of his arrows. The Hesperides offered no opposition to Atlas, for they were his daughters and happily allowed him to take the fruit he wanted.

Intoxicated with his new-found freedom, Atlas then tried to trick Heracles – 'Let me take the apples to the king,' he offered – thinking to leave the hero bearing the burden that had, until then, been his own.

Heracles was not so easily fooled, however, and asked Atlas to resume the load for a moment while he made himself more comfortable. But no sooner had the Titan taken the heavens on his shoulders again, than Heracles was off, leaving Atlas with the burden that he still bears, to this very day.

When Heracles presented himself before Eurystheus again, alive and well and bearing three golden fruits in his hand, the king was not pleased to see him. Eleven labours completed, including two journeys to the ends of the earth! Eurystheus was running out of ideas. He thought and thought, and at last hit upon a fiendishly cunning scheme. If Heracles could go to the ends of the earth and back, how would he feel about going to hell and back?

He began to plot Heracles twelfth and most terrible labour.

THE HOUND OF HELL

'Of late,' said the king, 'I have become concerned about the level of crime in Mycenae. What I really need is a good watchdog – the best one I know is Cerberus. Bring him to me, alive!'

To remove the stain of his sin, Heracles had no choice but to obey. Now this Cerberus was the most terrifying hound, for he had three heads and dripping jaws and great rolling eyes like saucers, and he guarded the gates to the Underworld, the kingdom of the god Hades. To accomplish this labour, Heracles would have to enter the realm of Death itself.

With the help of the god Hermes, guide of travellers and souls, Heracles made his way into the infernal regions, and after various obstacles and interruptions he stood at last before the throne of Hades. The Lord of the Dead agreed to allow Heracles to take Cerberus on one condition: that he should master him with neither club nor arrows, but with nothing more than his bare hands.

So it was that the son of Zeus and the Hound of Hell engaged in their contest of strength, and while the struggle raged you could not tell which was man and which was dog for all the growling and the howling and the grappling and the ripping and the twisting and the tearing. But at last Heracles was victorious, and he dragged Cerberus by the scruff of one of his necks all the way back to Mycenae.

When Heracles presented himself before Eurystheus again, with the hound of hell padding along behind him like some friendly puppy, Eurystheus grudgingly had to concede that he had no more quests to set before him, no more tasks for him to accomplish, and that he had completed the terms of his service. After twelve labours, the stain of his sin was removed and Heracles was free to go.

The hero continued to have many more adventures. In the end, he died at the innocent hands of his wife Deianeira, deceived by the lies of the centaur Nessus whom Heracles had killed when he tried to violate her. In his dying moments, Nessus had his revenge; his blood, he told Deianeira, was a love charm that would ensure her husband's unwavering affection. She took the blood he offered her and later, fearing that Heracles loved another, smeared it on his sacrificial shirt.

Making offerings by the altar, Heracles had not long put the shirt on when he felt a fire consuming his body from within, for the blood was like a spark to kindling. He howled in pain and tried to tear the garment off but it was stuck fast to his body, and as he pulled at the deadly cloth, he ripped skin from flesh and flesh from bone. Heracles, whom no living adversary had ever been able to kill, was dying through the trickery of a dead enemy.

According to his instructions, a funeral pyre of oak and wild olive was built and the great hero laid himself on it, with his club for his pillow and his lion skin for his blanket. At first, no one could bring himself to light the pyre, but at last, one by the name of Philoctetes kindled the fire, and in reward for this act of kindness Heracles bequeathed to him his quiver, his bow and his arrows.

The flames licked and crackled their way towards the dying hero, and the moment they reached his body a cloud descended from the sky and in a blaze of thunder and lightning Heracles was taken in glory into heaven. And there, in Olympus, he became one with the Immortals. Reconciled at last with his old enemy Hera, he married her daughter Hebe, and there he lives still, in the peace, beauty and eternal happiness of Paradise. And what man – or hero – could ask for more?

THE CURSE OF THE BULL

Looking down from his pinnacle on lofty Olympus, Zeus scanned the world, to see what he might see. And there, down in Phoenicia, picking flowers in a meadow by the shore, he saw the princess Europa – shining-faced Europa, the 'wide-eyed' one.

In the guise of a bull, Zeus descended to earth. Hearing a soft snort behind her, Europa turned and the prettiest sight met her eyes – a beautiful bull, with flanks and horns as white as ivory. Cautiously she approached the animal. It seemed as tame and playful as a kitten. She laughed with delight as the bull allowed her to stroke his nose and to garland his horns with flowers, and her delight increased even further when her charming pet bowed down and allowed her to climb on his back.

The beast rose and Europa called to her handmaidens – 'Look at me! I'm riding on the back of a bull!' The bull pranced around the meadow, with the laughing princess on its back, and then changed course, towards the sea, and before Europa could call 'Stop!', it had plunged into the frothing and foaming waves. On and on the bull surged through the rolling swell, swimming ever westward, with the terrified princess clinging to his horns, until at last they came ashore on the island of Crete.

And there, under a plane tree, the union of Europa and Zeus was consummated, and the child that she bore was called Minos, who would be king of Crete. And Europa of the wide eyes gave her name to this alien region to which Zeus had carried her: it was called Europe.

In the palace at Knossos on the island of Crete, King Minos sat with furrowed brow. His brothers, Rhadamanthys and Sarpedon, were disputing his right to the throne. What Minos needed was a sign, a portent, of his divine right to kingship. He went down to the shore and prayed to Poseidon, brother of Zeus; Poseidon, god of the sea.

'Lord Poseidon, master of the waves and ruler of the waters and of all that dwell there, hear my prayer. Send me a sea-gift as proof of my rightful kingship. Send me a bull from the sea, and I will offer it on the altar of sacrifice in your honour, and in gratitude to you.'

Hardly were the words out of his mouth than the wind rose and the waves began to churn as if stirred by some great force, and out of the realm of the sea king, out of the turquoise waters, there arose a magnificent bull, with flanks and horns as white as ivory, in every respect like the bull of Zeus who had abducted Europa, Minos' own mother. What a splendid beast it was, far too splendid, Minos thought, to die on the blade of sacrifice. And so he substituted another in its stead, foolishly believing that he could outwit the god.

But Poseidon was not deceived, and to punish Minos for his crime of disobedience, the god fixed his gaze on Pasiphaë, wife of Minos – shining-faced Pasiphaë, the 'all-illuminating' one – and fuelled in her a passionate desire for the white bull. Maddened with longing, Pasiphaë went to the cunning craftsman Daedalos.

'Fashion for me a disguise so that I may approach my beloved, and we may lie together, like with like.'

And clever Daedalos made the likeness of a cow, and the queen donned her disguise and behind this bovine mask approached the bull, the object of her desire, and the bull was deceived and mated with her.

And the fruit of this union was a monster, an abomination, a thing – a hideous, deformed creature with the head of a bull and the body of a man that none but a mother could love. And the creature was called the Minotaur, the 'Minos-bull'.

When King Minos heard what had happened, he paced the floor of his palace. Who would wish to be king, he thought, with all the trouble it brought? His foolish wife had, it seemed, become infatuated with – of all things – the bull sent by Poseidon, and

the end result of her unnatural amour was this half-creature, this Minotaur.

King Minos decided that the creature would have to be hidden away from prying eyes. He summoned Daedalos.

'I want you to build me a prison,' he commanded, 'in which to conceal the Minotaur – a prison from which he can never escape, and where human eyes may never penetrate.'

And clever Daedalos at once set to work to build a living tomb for the bull-man, and what he constructed was a vast maze, the like of which has never been seen before or since, with winding passages and spiralling ways and pathways that doubled back on themselves and dead-ends and dark corners, and in this tortuous prison the reviled Minotaur was incarcerated so that no one would see him, the loathly inhabitant in the heart of the palace at Knossos, on the blue-washed island of Crete.

On the quayside in the port of Athens, seven youths and seven maidens stood weeping and shivering with fear. They were bound for Knossos in a ship with black sails, Athens' eight-yearly tribute to the conqueror Minos in payment for the murder of his son Androgeus. Once there, they would be delivered to a flesh-eating monster in a maze.

But on this particular voyage, the third of its kind, there was one among their number of the most exalted birth; this was Theseus, son of Poseidon, and adopted son of Aegeus, king of Athens. Now Theseus had a secret mission. Among the company destined to be sacrificed to the Cretan bull, he would enter the labyrinth and there he would slay the monster, and thus set Athens free. If he met with success, he told Aegeus, he would hoist white sails on the returning ship; if he failed, the sails would be black.

When the victims arrived at Knossos, bold Theseus boasted of his parentage, proclaiming that he was the son of Poseidon, god of the sea.

'Prove it!' said Minos, irritated, and tossed a ring into the waters, telling Theseus to retrieve it. Whereupon Theseus dived in and brought back not only the ring but another trophy, too – the crown of Amphitrite, queen of the sea.

MINOAN CULTURE

KNOSSOS, NEAR present-day Iráklion in Crete, was the centre of the Minoan civilization which takes its name from King Minos, the legendary ruler of Knossos. Like Troy, Knossos and the tales of ancient Crete were once assumed to belong to the realm of fantasy. However, starting in 1899, the archaeologist Sir Arthur Evans began to excavate on the island and, over the next 35 years, laid bare to the eyes of the world the ancient Minoan civilization of which Homer had sung.

Evans divided this civilization into three main periods: early Minoan or Pre-palatial, c. 3000–2000 BCE; middle Minoan or Early Palatial, c. 2000–1600 BCE; and late Minoan or High Palatial c. 1600–1150 BCE. Its golden age was between the Middle and Late periods around 1600 BCE, when Minos was in power.

Dating from as early as 2000 BCE and spreading over 2½ hectares (5½ acres), the palace complex which Evans excavated showed that Knossos had been a highly important commercial and cultural centre. Among the finds were exquisite frescoes and fine pottery, as well as such sophisticated amenities as bathrooms, ventilation systems, conduits for water and chutes for waste-removal and, in the store-rooms, richly ornamented vessels that would have contained 85,500 litres (19,000 gallons) of olive oil, for use in this one palace alone. Such evidence pointed to a lifestyle of great wealth and opulence. Objects of foreign origin, especially Egyptian pottery dating to specific Pharoanic times, were proof of the Minoans' role as successful traders.

The maze-like layout of the palace, the image of a labyrinth depicted on a corridor, and the youths and girls performing a bull-leaping ritual in the frescoes on the walls, all hinted at some historical basis for the legend of the Minotaur.

What happened to end this splendid civilization is not known for sure. An earthquake in around 1400 BCE may have started the final decline, or there may have been a war – or even a combination of the two, with invaders taking advantage of the instability that would have occurred after a natural disaster such as an earthquake.

Watching this show of bravado was the princess Ariadne, daughter of Minos and half-sister to the Minos-bull, and she was greatly taken with this handsome stranger from Athens. Catching her gaze, Theseus approached her and placed on her head the crown from the sea, and Ariadne's fate was sealed. Her heart filled with such love for Theseus that she was prepared to betray her own father to save him.

Ariadne knew that her beloved was destined to be devoured by the Minotaur and was desperate to help him escape, but could not think of a way. So, like her mother before her, she turned to Daedalos and asked for his assistance. And what did clever Daedalos give Ariadne to aid her lover in his quest? A sword with a sharp, slitting edge? An axe that would sever sinew from sinew and bone from bone? A dagger to plunge secretly and silently into flesh? No, what the wizard-craftsman gave her was nothing more than a simple ball of twine.

Theseus took the twine and, securing one end at the entrance, made his way into the labyrinth, unravelling the thread as he went, until at last he arrived in the chamber where the Minotaur lurked. There was not a second to lose – the element of surprise was all – and before the bull-man could gather his strength, before he had time to grasp what was happening, Theseus had plunged his dagger deep into his heart and killed the master of the maze.

Quickly, the hero fingered his way back along the thread of fate, back through the twists and turns of the labyrinth, and out into the open air, where Ariadne was waiting. Having deceived her father, the princess could no longer remain in Knossos and, accompanied by her sister Phaedra, she fled Crete with Theseus and set sail with him for Athens.

Down in the labyrinth of Knossos, Daedalos and his son Icarus were languishing. King Minos had discovered the part played by the master-craftsman in the affair of Pasiphaë and the sea-bull, and had decided to punish him by placing him in the very prison he had designed for someone else.

'You're so clever, aren't you?' the king raged. 'First you make a cow costume for my besotted wife, and then you help my daughter betray me and escape with the Athenians. None of this would have happened if it weren't for you! You made the labyrinth – you live in it!'

The irony of his solution appealed to the king's sense of humour, and went some way to assuage his anger. Meanwhile, in the maze fashioned to his own design, Daedalos was working towards his escape. He had managed to secrete some useful materials – a pile of feathers, some wire, some thread, some wax – and with these he fashioned two pairs of wings, one for himself and one for his son, that would allow them, once out of their prison, to soar away to freedom, past the soldiers guarding the palace, past the ships guarding the ports.

On a framework of wire, he secured the first row of feathers, attaching the quills to the frame with twists of wire and twine. Working methodically, he added row upon row – securing the whole with wax – until he had completed his task and two pairs of perfect angel-like wings lay before him.

He slipped his pair on, and lowered the other pair over his son's shoulders.

'When we are free of the maze,' he warned Icarus, 'fly neither so low that the sea wets your wings, nor so high that the sun melts them, but steer a middle course,' and with these words of caution he soared up and out of the labyrinth, his son following close behind.

It was not long before Crete was no more than a speck of brown in the expanse of sea below them. Soon they had left the islands of Naxos, Delos and Paros behind on their left, and Lebynthos and Calymne on their right. What a sensation it was to fly like a bird! Icarus swooped and dived like an airborne acrobat, skimming the thermals and propelled by a fresh breeze in the boundless blue of the sky. In all his young years, he had never experienced anything so wonderful. The excitement of it went to his head and he forgot his father's words and rose higher and higher towards the burning sun.

When Daedalos looked back to see if his son was still following, all he saw was an empty space where Icarus had been. Then he looked down at the sea below and saw feathers, hundreds of white feathers, floating on the water like flotsam from a wreck. He knew at once what had happened: Icarus had flown too near the sun so that it had melted the wax in his wings, and he had plummeted to his death.

The body of Icarus was washed ashore on a nearby island, and Daedalos buried it there. And ever afterwards, the island bore his son's name: it was called Icaria.

Down on the island of Naxos, Ariadne, all alone, was weeping. Halfway through the voyage home to Athens, Theseus had decided to drop anchor at the island and Ariadne, exhausted after the trials of the labyrinth, had lain down on the shore and fallen asleep. And while she was sleeping, Theseus betrayed her. Careless of all she had done for him, he set sail without her, leaving Ariadne abandoned, desolate and alone.

But her plight did not go unnoticed, for up in Olympus Dionyos the bull-god and son of Zeus had seen her, and came to undo the wrong that Theseus had done, for he made Ariadne his bride and set her by his side in heaven and placed on her head a golden crown of stars, so that she became known as Aridela, the 'one who shines from afar'. And her beauty still shines out of the northern sky, in the constellation known as the Corona Borealis, the 'crown of the north'.

Meanwhile, on a clifftop in Athens, King Aegeus had been anxiously waiting for his son's return, looking out for a glimpse of a white sail that would signal the success of his quest. But Theseus, careless of Ariadne, was also careless of his father for in the excitement of victory he had forgotten to change the sails, as he had promised he would. So when Aegeus, screening his old eyes against the sun as he scanned the horizon, saw a ship with black sails, he believed his son to be dead and threw himself from the cliff, and his lifeless body sank to the bottom of the sea where it became food for the fishes.

In the palace of Athens, Theseus, now king, sat harbouring thoughts of revenge. His wife and queen, Phaedra – whom he had married after abandoning her sister Ariadne – was dead. And the cause? A note from her had revealed all. Hippolytus, his own son by Antiope, had violated Phaedra and she, in shame, had hanged herself.

The truth was altogether different. Phaedra had developed an incestuous and obsessive passion for Hippolytus, and when her advances were rejected, she punished him by ending her own life so that he would be blamed for a crime he had not committed.

Theseus was totally deceived, and ordered Hippolytus to leave Athens at once. But the more the king brooded, the greater his anger grew, so he went down to the shore, like Minos before him, and prayed to his father Poseidon, god of the sea.

'Lord Poseidon, Master of the Waves, hear my prayer. Avenge the crime that has been done. Send a beast in the path of Hippolytus.'

Hardly were the words out of his mouth than the wind rose and the waves began to churn as if stirred by some great force, and out of the realm of the sea king, out of the turquoise waters, there arose a magnificent bull, with flanks and horns as white as ivory, in every respect like the bull of Zeus who had abducted Europa, in every respect like the bull of Poseidon who was father to the Minotaur. And the wave with the bull on its crest washed across the path of Hippolytus, who was riding away from Athens, and panicked the horses pulling his chariot, so that he fell and was dragged to his death.

And so this sad tale has come full circle, with a white bull from the sea at the beginning and a white bull from the sea at the end, and may we all be the wiser for the hearing of it.

JASON AND THE GOLDEN FLEECE

There was once a king by the name of Pelias, who ruled Iolcus in Thessaly. Pelias, however, had not come by the throne by honest means for he had wrested it from his half-brother Aeson, who now lived as a prisoner in the palace.

Expecting all other men to live by his own villain's code, Pelias was forever watchful, waiting for the one who might do to him what he had done to his brother. To add to his sense of insecurity, a prophecy had been made which haunted him by day and by night. At banquets, at royal audiences, at the hunt, in wakefulness and in dreams, it would steal into his mind like a thief in the night, unbidden, unwanted and unwelcome. The prophecy had been given him by an oracle, and it was this:

'Beware the man of the race of Aeolus, the man who wears only one sandal.'

From that moment on, Pelias, obsessive and suspicious, developed an unnatural interest in footwear.

Now it so happened that Aeson had a wife by the name of Polymele, who one day bore him a baby son called Diomedes. Knowing that Pelias would kill this child for fear that he might later claim the throne, Polymele pretended that the babe was still-born, and had her women wail and howl over the swaddled bundle. By this deceit, she managed to save her child's life, and had him smuggled out of the city to Mount Pelion, there to be cared for and tutored by the centaur Chiron.

The boy grew up in this mountain wilderness, and learned many things from his teacher – how to ride, how to hunt, how to use weapons, how to play music. At last, when the time came for him to put away boyish freedoms and accept the responsibilities of a man, he said farewell to Chiron, donned a leather tunic, threw a leopard's skin over his shoulder, took a spear in each hand, placed a pair of sandals on his feet, and set off for Iolcus.

He had not gone far when he came to a broad, swollen stream, and there on the bank stood a frail old woman, wringing her hands and weeping for she wished to cross but was afraid.

'Good day to you,' said the young man courteously, 'Allow me to help you. I shall carry you to the other side.' And so saying, he lifted her onto his back and waded into the water.

Now at first glance, the old woman had seemed to be very small and thin – no more than a bundle of bones – but the deeper they went, the heavier she seemed to get, and the tighter she clung on to him, almost squeezing the breath out of him. Struggling with the increasing burden on his back and the ever-wilder swirling of the current around his legs, he almost lost his footing and found, when he reached the other bank, that one sandal had come off and was, he imagined, still stuck somewhere in the mud of the stream-bed. But he could walk as easily with one as with two, so he did not trouble to find the lost shoe. In any case, he had a more pressing problem – to relieve himself of his heavy burden.

As he carefully lowered his passenger on to the ground, he was amazed to see her metamorphose from the bent old crone she had been only moments before into a tall, stately and magnificent figure. The old woman he had borne across the stream was none other than the goddess Hera herself. From that day on, Hera was his ally.

The young man proceeded to Iolcus and, once there, presented himself to King Pelias. The king looked him over. He saw a tall, handsome stranger with long hair waving down to his broad shoulders. In his hands were two broad-bladed spears. On his shoulder was a leopard's skin. On his body was a close-fitting leather tunic. And on his feet was a single sandal. Trying to keep the tremor out of his voice, Pelias demanded to know who the stranger was.

'What is your name? What do you want here? Why have you come?' he barked.

'I am of the race of Aeolus, the son of Aeson and the foster-child of Chiron. I was once known as Diomedes, but Chiron called me Jason. Jason is my name, and I have come to claim the throne.'

This was the moment that Pelias had been dreading all these years. Well, oracle or no oracle, he had managed to hold on to his title all this time, and he had no intention of handing it over now to some ill-shod young man who had come marching into his city. How could he even be sure that this Jason was who he said he was? The situation called for the greatest guile.

'Diomedes – or rather Jason, my boy! How delighted I am to see you. We all thought you were dead! What a wonderful surprise to find you still living. Welcome, welcome, dear nephew.'

The king's effusiveness oozed like honey from the comb.

'Greetings to you, uncle,' Jason replied, and continued, 'As my father's brother, you will know that the throne is mine by right. However, I do not wish to deprive you of all the benefits of kingship which you have so long enjoyed. You may keep for yourself all the flocks and herds that go with the title, but the throne itself you must relinquish to me.'

'Well said, well said, a fair bargain, is it not?' blustered the king, darting a look at the others assembled there as if all were complicit in this charade. 'I am, as you can see, an old and weary man and the burdens of kingship, alas, hang heavy on my shoulders. I would willingly give up the throne to a younger heir. But you know, my boy' – and here his tone became whispered and conspiratorial – 'the crown belongs only to one who is fit to wear it. To prove yourself worthy of the honour, I fancy a little quest would be in order. To earn the throne of Iolcus you must first bring me the Golden Fleece.'

The Golden Fleece of which the king spoke was famed far and wide, but had a sad history. Many years before, Phrixus and Helle, the two children of King Athamas of Boeotia and descendants of Aeolus, found their lives in danger and had to flee their homeland. The pair escaped on the back of a magic ram given them by the god Hermes, the traveller's guide. The ram had a fleece of gold, could speak and reason, and could fly through the air as easily as it could run on land. Clinging to its gilded wool, brother and sister soared away eastwards but, as they were crossing the straits between Thrace and Phrygia, Helle lost her grip and plunged to her death in the sea below; and in her honour the spot was forever after known as the Hellespont. Brokenhearted, Phrixus continued his journey and finally alighted in Colchis, on the eastern shores of the Black Sea, where he sacrificed the ram to Zeus. The wonderful fleece he gave to Aeëtes, king of the country, who suspended it from an oak tree in the Grove of Ares, where it was guarded by a dragon that never slept.

This was the challenge that Pelias now set before Jason, and which Jason boldly accepted: to make the long voyage to Colchis, to confront the unsleeping dragon, and to seize the Golden Fleece. It was a challenge which the king, privately, hoped would end in Jason's death. Publicly, of course, he made much show of wishing his nephew every success.

The call immediately went out for volunteers to join Jason in his quest, and those who answered it included in their number the bravest and best in all the world. There was Heracles, strong man of Boeotia; there were Castor and Pollux the Dioscuri, sons of Zeus and Leda, and Meleager, slayer of the Calydonian boar; there were Calais and Zetes, the winged sons of Boreas, the North Wind; there was the hero Peleus, father of the great Achilles; there were Acastus, son of King Pelias and, some say, Theseus the bull-slayer of Athens; there was Orpheus the poet, master of the enchanted lyre, and many other heroes, too. Never before or since has such a gallant company been gathered together.

Meanwhile, a great ship had been built for the voyage. She was fashioned of seasoned timber taken from the trees on Mount Pelion, and was fitted with fifty oars. Athene herself had added a beam to her prow, cut from the oracular oak of Zeus at Dodona. She was called the *Argo*, and her crew the Argonauts.

At last the *Argo* was ready to sail, and all came down to the shore to witness her departure, including Pelias.

'A fair wind speed you, and may the gods smile on you,' were his lying words of farewell.

Jason offered a prayer to Zeus, and threw mead into the sea from a golden goblet. Then Orpheus picked up his lyre and, as the Argonauts swung their oars in time to the enchanted rhythm of his music and a gentle breeze filled the sails, the mighty vessel sliced its way into the limpid Aegean waters, towards whatever adventures the gods willed.

After a long time or a short time, Jason and his Argonauts sighted land – a jagged cape jutting out into the water. Over the cliffs strange, flying forms dived and whirled like wild sea-birds, the beating of their wings thrumming like thunder and their eerie cries howling like the wind. Dropping anchor and disembarking to investigate further, the Argonauts realized that these spectres were none other than the loathsome Harpies, the three spirit-sisters of the tempest who had the heads and breasts of women but the wings of birds, and went by the names of Ocypeta the Rapid, Celeno the Black, and Aello the Stormy. They appeared to be tormenting a blind old man who sat, crown on head, trying to eat a meal placed before him. Every time he was on the point of placing a morsel in his mouth, one of the Harpies would swoop down, seize it in her talons, and make away with it.

Calais and Zetes, the sons of the North Wind, instantly spread their great wings and – with the other Argonauts forming a shield behind them – chased the tormentors away.

'Oh, my boy, thank you, thank you!' cried King Phineus – for that was the old man's name – as he gripped Jason's hand in his shaky old fingers. 'I am feeble in body but not in mind, and I have seen many things in my time, so – tell where me where you are going, and I may be able to advise you.'

When Jason explained his quest and the route he would have to follow, Phineus threw up his hands in horror.

'Not through the Symplegades! Not through the Clashing Rocks! They will crush your ship to splinters! But there is a way … listen …' And he whispered words of advice to Jason which Jason took care to remember as they all boarded the *Argo* again and set sail.

After a long time or a short time, the Argonauts sighted what all sailors dreaded – the Symplegades of which Phineus had spoken. These were two huge rocks that jutted out of the sea like great towers. Only a small passage lay between them and whenever a ship tried to make its way through, the rocks would spin on their bases and come crashing together, crushing the vessel to powder like grain between two grindstones.

Silence fell on the *Argo* as all on board gazed ahead. There stood the Symplegades, barring the way forward … still and ominous … waiting. Jason ordered the crew to row as close to the rocks as they could and then, remembering the advice of Phineus, released a dove from among those kept on board. The bird flew forward and, as the rocks sensed its approach, they shivered, tottered, swivelled, moved inwards and collided. Then they began to pull apart again as if drawing breath for the next assault. Quickly, as a few tail feathers from the escaping dove fluttered down, the Argonauts rowed the ship through before the rocks had time to crash together again.

Out in open waters once more, they embraced and cheered. They had overcome this particular terror of the seas. They had overcome the Symplegades.

At last, the *Argo* arrived at her destination – Colchis and the kingdom of Aeëtes. Jason presented himself before the king and announced that he wished for the Golden Fleece.

Now whatever Jason's rights, by way of ancient kinship, might or might not have been to the fleece that once belonged to Phrixus, Aeëtes fancied a little sport with the stranger who now stood before him.

'So you want the Golden Fleece?' the wily old king began. 'Well, young man, the prize is yours for the taking, but only if you can perform two simple little tasks. Yoke my bulls and plough the Field of Ares and then sow the field with dragon's teeth.'

No one, Aeëtes was certain, could carry out these tasks and live. Still, it would be amusing to watch the stranger die a horrible death in attempting them. However, there was one factor the king had not taken into account in his calculations: the power of love.

All this time, looking down from their pinnacle on Olympus, Athene and Hera had been watching the progress of their protégé Jason, and they decided he needed a little help. So they approached Aphrodite and asked her to persuade her son Eros, the god of love, to intervene.

Now among the company surrounding Aeëtes was his daughter, the princess Medea, and it was her heart at which the love-god aimed his arrow. As the bolt hit its mark, Medea felt as if startled awake from a deep sleep. She saw Jason standing before her – indeed he was all she saw. What had been the matter with her? Why had she not noticed before how hand-some he was? And under the spell of Eros, Medea fell hopelessly head over heels in love.

As soon as she could, she sought Jason out privately, and offered to help him on condition that he take her away with him, and so the bargain was struck, Jason swearing an oath to the gods that he would be faithful to Medea forever.

Now Medea was the perfect ally to have in times of trouble, for she was the niece of the great enchantress Circe and had, herself, great knowledge of herbs and ointments and charms and witcheries. To aid Jason in his task, she gave him a phial containing an enchanted potion made from the crocus that had sprung from the blood of Prometheus. Jason smeared the potion over his body, his shield and his spear and thus – veiled by magic – prepared to yoke the bulls.

Under his hand, these ferocious beasts, with hooves of brass and breath of fire, proved as docile as lambs, and Jason easily harnessed them and ploughed the field, although it did take him all day.

King Aeëtes looked on in wonder. He had been convinced that Jason would have been burned, if not gored, to death by the bulls. But there were still the dragon's teeth …

These teeth had belonged to a dragon killed by Cadmus, founder of the city of Thebes, and they had some unusual properties.

Night was coming on and a full moon was in the sky as Jason prepared to sow the furrows he had ploughed. Moving up and down the field, he scattered the teeth into the turned earth, covering them over as he went, until all had been sown.

At first, all remained peaceful and still in the silver light of the moon, but then, down below the surface of the soil, something began to stir. Spearheads pricked up through the earth like little shoots, then the earth began to heave, and in no time at all an army of warriors had sprouted and stood in rows, tall and straight, like stands of corn. Seeing Jason, they raised a mighty battle cry and rushed towards him, but Jason threw a stone into their midst so that the warriors, each thinking he been attacked by his brothers, fell to fighting amongst themselves and such was the slaughter on the Field of Ares that night that in the end all the dragon-warriors lay dead.

This, of course, was not the outcome that Aeëtes had either planned or expected, and he now refused to hand over the Golden Fleece, as promised.

'You did not seriously believe I would allow you to take such a treasure away with you? My dear boy …' he mockingly said to an angry Jason, 'I spoke in jest!'

Well, Jason thought, if the Fleece could not be obtained honourably, it would have to be taken dishonourably. Here again, it was Medea who came to his aid.

Without her father knowing, Medea secretly led Jason to the Grove of Ares and the oak tree where hung the Golden Fleece. The splendour of this luxurious pelt was enough to rival all the gold in the coffers of Midas, but it was impossible to come close to it because of the dragon who guarded it, twined in a thousand coils around the tree and closely observing the intruders while it hissed and rumbled threateningly.

Medea, fearless, stealthily approached the dragon and began to croon an incantation. The monster appeared soothed. Medea then sprinkled the dragon's eyes with a magic concoction of juniper. Its lids fluttered, wavered and closed and, after aeons of sleepless nights and days, the guardian of the Golden Fleece finally fell into a deep and unshakeable slumber.

At once, Jason removed the Fleece from the tree, and the pair made off for the waiting *Argo* with its crew of Argonauts, taking with them Medea's half-brother Apsyrtus. Naturally, it did not take long for news of their flight to reach the ears of King Aeëtes, and he at once embarked with his men in hot pursuit.

Love is blind to reason and it was at this point that Medea abandoned not only reason but kindness, too. Seeing her father's ship closing in on the *Argo*, she killed her half-brother, chopped his body up, and flung the pieces into the sea, which Aeëtes was obliged to collect, one by one, so that his son might have a proper burial, and in this way she helped Jason make good his escape.

During the return voyage to Iolcus, the *Argo* passed by the islands of the Sirens, bird-women whose enchanted singing was so irresistible that sailors would fling themselves into the sea to reach them, only to meet their deaths on the islands' rocks. But Orpheus, picking up his lyre, out-sang the Sirens, so that the Argonauts were deaf to their seductions.

At last, they achieved the shores of Iolcus where Jason learned, to his sorrow, that during his long absence both his father and mother, Aeson and Polymele, and his infant brother Promachus, born while he was away, had died. Faced with a choice between murder by Pelias and taking their own lives, Aeson and Polymele had chosen suicide. As for the infant, Pelias had dashed his brains out on the palace floor.

There is a darkness in the affairs of kings, one villainous deed feeding another, one rivalry inviting another's revenge, until the whole spirals down in a maelstrom of evil, and so it was with Pelias, Jason and Medea, who now found themselves face-to-face within the walls of Iolcus.

To avenge the deaths of Jason's parents, Medea prepared a large pot, a magic Cauldron of Regeneration so she said. She then persuaded the daughters of Pelias to kill their father, cut him up, and set the pieces to boil in the cauldron, whereupon – and this was the wonder of it, she insisted – they would all come together again and the king would step from the stewpot, as hale and whole as before. Eager to witness this marvellous marvel, the daughters of Pelias did exactly as she told them.

Of course, the mutilated fragments of the king's body did not become whole again but continued to bubble away until nothing was left of them but bare bones. But then Medea knew this all along.

Jason, meanwhile, went to Boeotia where he hung the Golden Fleece in the temple of Zeus, for Boeotia was its home. But winning the fleece did not, after all, bring him the throne of Iolcus. Fearing the vengeance of Acastus, the son of Pelias, for the murder of his father – that same Acastus who had sailed with him on the Argo – Jason relinquished his claim and made a hasty departure, with Medea, bound for Corinth.

Here they found the throne vacant, and Medea claimed it since it had once belonged to her father Aeëtes. She and Jason became king and queen of Corinth and ruled for ten prosperous years, producing a total of seven sons and seven daughters.

But there is a darkness in the affairs of kings, and so it was that Jason came to suspect Medea of poisoning the former ruler of Corinth, and on these grounds told her that he was abandoning her in favour of the princess Glauce. This Jason proposed, despite the oath he had sworn back in Colchis always to be faithful to Medea, despite the fact that he owed his kingship to her. Foolish Jason, thus to cross a witch!

Medea made no protestations, but quietly sent a magnificent robe as a wedding gift to the new bride, to be worn at her nuptial feast. As soon as Glauce put it on it burst into flames, consuming not only her but all those present – all that is, except Jason, who escaped.

It was rumoured that Medea then cut the throats of her children, or sacrificed them; others recount how they were stoned to death by the Corinthians in revenge for the murder of Glauce. Whatever the truth of the matter, it is known that Hera took their souls and made them immortal. When her end came, Medea, too, became immortal and took up residence in the Elysian Fields, the happy-ever-after land of the Blessed.

As for Jason, who had broken his oath to the gods when he abandoned Medea, he became a sad and sorry figure, wandering the world alone, homeless and hated. When at last old age overtook him, when his once-thick locks were sparse and white, when his once-proud body was frail and bent, he returned to Corinth, a nameless vagabond, unknown and unsung.

There on the shore he saw an old friend. It was the *Argo*, and he sat awhile, resting his back against her familiar hull, and mused on the past with all its triumphs and tragedies. And as he sat there, deep in his reverie, kind Death came to him, for the prow of the ship loosened itself and fell on him, crushing his skull.

As for the *Argo* herself – that great ship which had seen so many adventures and had borne on her boards the bravest and the best – as for her, the sea-god Poseidon took her and placed her image amongst the stars, for she was innocent of all blame.

THE TROJAN WAR

On high ground surrounded by fields of corn, where two rivers converge and where Phrygia looks westward to Thrace, there – safe within sturdy walls – once stood the city of Ilium, the fabled city of Troy. But the glory of Troy was long, long ago, before the warlike Achaens came in their ships from across the sea and laid siege to the city and razed it to the ground, wiping it from the face of the earth and almost from memory, so that for generations to come people would say it was no more than a dream in the minds of the bards.

This is the story of Troy, and this is how it all began.

There was once a king by the name of Priam and he ruled the city of Troy. Priam's wife was called Hecabe and one day, shortly before she was due to deliver the child she was carrying, she had a nightmare. She dreamt that she had given birth to a bundle of sticks out of which fiery serpents darted. She awoke screaming in terror. The king at once consulted a seer who told him what the dream meant.

'He that is soon to be born will bring ruin on Troy! Kill him or the city will fall!'

By this time, the infant – a boy child – had been delivered, but Priam could not bring himself to murder his newborn son, so he passed the task of infanticide to his chief herdsman Agelaus. Agelaus took the swaddled babe and left him on Mount Ida, exposed to the elements and to whatever wild beasts might happen by. But on visiting the site five days later, the herdsman was amazed to find the baby he had left to perish not only alive but positively thriving! In the interval, a she-bear had come to suckle the babe and this had sustained him. Taking this as a powerful omen, Agelaus rescued the infant from the rock and took him home, carrying him in a bag, after which he named him: thenceforth the child was known as 'Paris'.

Paris grew up alongside the herdsman's own son, and learned all there was to know about herding and the care of cattle. But despite his humble station, the blood of kings ran in his veins and his nobility soon became apparent in his beauty, strength, valour and quickness of mind, which seemed to increase daily. Such natural charms did not go unnoticed, and it was not long before Paris became the beloved of the nymph Oenone, daughter of the river-god Oeneus. Together they would hunt, and together they would herd the cattle, in those blissful days of innocence before everything changed.

The gods had noticed the charms of Paris too, and they were about to take a hand in his life that would alter it forever.

The Judgement of Paris

While mortals were going about their daily business, up on Olympus a celebration was in full swing – the wedding of the sea-goddess Thetis and the mortal Peleus, king of the Myrmidons. All the gods and goddesses had been invited to the feast except one – Eris, or Discord. In fury, Eris forced her way into the midst of the merry-making throng and threw down her challenge. It was a golden apple, to be awarded to the fairest among those present.

Without hesitating, Hera stooped to pick it up.

'My dear,' said Athene behind her, 'I think that apple is mine. Everyone knows that I am the fairest of the Olympians.'

'No, no,' came Aphrodite's voice. 'You are both mistaken! My beauty is famed far and wide. The prize is mine.'

As the disagreement between the three goddesses threatened to turn into an ugly quarrel, Zeus intervened and said that someone other than they, someone who was not an Olympian, should judge the contest. And that is why, as Paris was quietly tending the herd on the remote pastures of the mountains, he suddenly found himself face to face with three of the greatest goddesses on Olympus.

'Award the apple to me,' whispered Hera to Paris, drawing herself up to her fulsome magnificence, 'and I will make you lord of all Asia and the richest man alive.'

'Award the apple to me,' whispered Athene, her shining eyes flashing, 'and I will make you victorious in all your battles, and wise beyond all other men.'

'Award the apple to me,' whispered Aphrodite, sidling up to Paris with such voluptuous seductiveness that it made his head spin, 'and I will give you the most beautiful woman in all the world as your wife.'

There was no question as to the identity of this paragon, for it was well known that Helen of Sparta was the fairest woman alive. The goddess's offer would have tempted even the sternest of men; there was, however, a small drawback.

'But she's married!' cried Paris. 'To King Menelaus!'

Laughing her tinkling laugh, Aphrodite pinched his cheek playfully.

'Oh, you sweet, old-fashioned boy!' she exclaimed. 'What is a mere marriage knot to one such as I? Am I not the goddess of love?'

The merest nudge had been all Paris needed to come to the decision he had already all but made, and so, without further ado, he awarded the Apple of Discord to Aphrodite, earning himself a flurry of kisses from her and the enduring enmity of Hera and Athene.

Thus the small matter of a forgotten wedding invitation set in motion an unstoppable train of events that would lead to disaster – but then it is on such trivia that the fates of men turn.

THE YOUTH OF HELEN

Now this Helen whom Aphrodite intended for Paris had a curious history, for her birth was not as that of other mortals'. Looking down from his pinnacle on lofty Olympus, Zeus, with his roving eye, had spotted her mother Leda bathing in a pool, and had seduced her in the form of a swan. Enfolded in the bird's white wings, Leda conceived; and that night, enfolded in the arms of her husband Tyndareus, she conceived again.

The result of this double conception was not, as you might expect, two bonny babes, but two large, smooth, glistening eggs. And when they cracked, what emerged were not two downy cygnets, but two pairs of twins, a boy and girl in each. From one egg came Helen and Pollux, the children of Zeus; from the other, Clytemnestra and Castor, the children of Tyndareus. The two boys, Castor and Pollux, were both accepted as his sons by Zeus, and became known as the Dioscuri. As for the sisters, Helen and Clytemnestra, they were marked from the start, for Aphrodite, angry at Tyndareus for failing to make proper offerings to her, had proclaimed that his daughters would be notorious for their adulteries – a prophecy that in Helen's case, she would later ensure with her bribe to Paris.

When Helen was only ten years old, there was a foretaste of the trouble to come, for she was abducted by Theseus, and had to be brought home again by her brothers, Castor and Pollux. The fame of her beauty spread far and wide, and when she grew to marriageable age she was besieged by princes wishing for her hand. The palace at Sparta, of which her father Tyndareus was king, overflowed with so many suitors – each trying to outvie the other with his gifts of gold and jewels – that they outnumbered the royal staff. Fearing that the suitors would later set to warring amongst themselves, Tyndareus set a condition before them: he would choose one amongst them to marry his beautiful daughter but first, he said, they must all swear an oath: they must promise that, should her future husband ever be in need of them, they would come to his aid. The suitors all swore, and then the king chose Menelaus, who married Helen with all due ceremony and celebration.

THE ELOPEMENT OF HELEN

Meanwhile, across the sea to the east, Paris – who had only recently awarded the apple to Aphrodite – was about to embark on the course of action set out for him by fate.

Now Priam had never forgotten his son and every year, as was the custom then, funeral games were held in his honour. This particular year, the king sent to his herdsman Agelaus for the finest bull in the herd to be given as a prize. Paris, who had up to now led a quiet rural life, longed for the excitement of the city, and begged Agelaus to be allowed to accompany him to Troy. The latter could see no harm in this proposition, and agreed.

Naturally, Paris could not resist joining in the games, and, hardened as he was by an outdoor life, he won every one of them, defeating his brothers – all fifty of them – who did not know who he was. Angered at such public humiliation, they were about to put him to the sword, when Agelaus cried out:

'Stay your hands! Kill him not! This is the son of Priam, whom you thought to be dead.'

The king could hardly believe what he was hearing, but managed to stagger to his feet and came over to embrace Paris.

'Oh, my boy,' he cried, the tears brimming in his eyes, 'you do not know what joy you bring into an old man's life. Welcome home – a thousand welcomes!'

But when the seers heard that Paris was returned, they again warned the king, as they had at the prince's birth:

'He that has come among us will bring ruin on Troy! Kill him or the city will fall!'

But having put Paris to death once – as he had thought – Priam refused to do it a second time, and would not heed the seers' words.

'What matters it if Troy should fall?' he proclaimed in a haze of euphoria. 'Do you not see? – my beloved son is returned to me, he who was lost has been found.' And the king ordered a great banquet to be laid out, with all the finest viands and sweetmeats and wine, to celebrate the homecoming of Paris.

But Paris had not forgotten Aphrodite's promise and as soon as he could, he persuaded his father – on some false pretext – to allow him to sail with a fleet to Sparta where the lovely Helen lived.

Paris was most hospitably received at the court of Menelaus, and the king feasted him for nine days. It was at the king's table that Paris first laid eyes on Helen. He was entranced. He had never seen such beauty before. He drank it in with every glance, like a man who seeks to quench a raging thirst and cares not that the chalice is poisoned. Helen, in her turn, was greatly taken with this handsome stranger. No voice was needed to express the rush of emotion that they experienced, for their eyes spoke all the words they needed. The more they looked, the more they loved, and the more they loved, the more they longed, and so they came to a secret and silent understanding, with barely a dozen words passing between them.

Under the cover of night, when Menelaus's attention was elsewhere, Helen fled with Paris down to the waiting ships and out to sea. It was at the island of Cranaë, their first port of call on their voyage to Ilium, that Helen of Sparta gave herself to Paris of Troy, fully, freely and lovingly.

THE SACRIFICE OF IPHIGENIA

When Menelaus discovered that his wife had eloped with his Trojan guest, he rallied all the kings and princes of the city states of Achaea, as this part of Greece was known, reminding them of the oath they had sworn to come to his aid when he needed them. A huge force of soldiers and ships was marshalled, ready to go to war to avenge the injury done to him. At their head was Agamemnon, high king of Mycenae, brother to Menelaus, and brother-in-law to Helen for he had married Helen's sister, Clytemnestra.

There, too, was Odysseus, king of Ithaca, who had joined the expedition with the greatest reluctance. A seer had warned him that, should he go to war, he would not see Ithaca for another twenty years. He had feigned madness to avoid the call, but had been found out and stood here now, as sane and sagacious a man as he had ever been.

Ajax, brave-hearted and of giant stature, was there, as was Nestor, the old king and wise counsellor. Patroclus was there, and by his side was his dearest friend Achilles, the most illustrious warrior in all the land and king of the Myrmidons of Thessaly.

How ironic are the circlings of fate, for this Achilles was none other than the son of Thetis and Peleus, who at their nuptials had omitted to invite Eris, whose Apple of

Discord contained the seeds of this present difficulty. When Achilles was no more than an infant, his divine mother, wishing to make him immortal, had dipped him in the river Styx, that stream that flows nine times around the land of the dead; the only part of the child that remained dry was the heel by which she held him, and so his heel remained the only part of him vulnerable to death.

Here, then, at Aulis in the narrow strait between Euboea and the mainland, was gathered a vast fleet of the finest and the best in all of Greece, ready for the long voyage north-eastward across the Aegean Sea to Troy. Ready, that is, but unable to move because of the fierce gale raging about them. It would have torn the sails to shreds, and ripped the mast from the decks. What could be the cause of such a savage wind?

Then it was remembered that Agamemnon had, on a recent hunt, killed a stag sacred to the goddess Artemis. It was Artemis whose displeasure was expressed in the storm. The goddess must be propiated and the only way to do that, a soothsayer assured the king, was to offer her the life of his daughter Iphigenia – a virgin princess to a virgin goddess. Agamemnon was horrified and knew that his wife Clytemnestra would die herself before she consented to the sacrifice of their child; but the Greek army was on the point of dispersing and if a remedy was not found soon the whole enterprise would collapse. So Agamemnon sent for Iphigenia on the pretence that he wished to marry her to Achilles.

Finding his name abused in this way, Achilles wished to protect the princess, but brave Iphigenia offered her neck to the axe and prepared to die for Greece. But just as the blade was about to fall, a cloud descended to envelop the princess and spirit her away to the temple of Artemis at Tauris, leaving a hind in her place. The gale ceased, a fair wind filled the sails, and a thousand ships embarked for Ilium, and Helen.

THE REFUSAL OF ACHILLES

On reaching their destination, Agamemnon sent to Priam to ask for the return of Helen. The old king, however, refused, either because he wished to keep her at Troy, or because she had not yet arrived in the city at that point, being still on the high seas with Paris. This denial was to instigate a war that would last for ten years before reaching its culmination.

Unable to breach the city walls, the Greeks set up camp outside Troy and besieged it, while the Trojans remained imprisoned within. Although they could not take Troy itself, the Greeks did manage to conquer many of its neighbouring allies, and divided the spoils amongst themselves. To Achilles fell a female captive by the name of Briseis; to Agamemnon fell Chryseis, daughter of a priest of Apollo. When the father of Chryseis came to beg for her release, Agamemnon refused. The priest then prayed to his god, whereupon Apollo let loose a hail of poisonous arrows that brought such plague and pestilence to the Greeks that at last Agamemnon was forced to release the girl to her father – but he did so with little grace and most grudgingly. Brooding on this small defeat, he began to feel cheated, deprived and demeaned. He, Agamemnon, high king of Mycenae and commander-in-chief of the force that now besieged Troy, had been made to give up his prize, while other, lesser men continued to enjoy theirs. And so, in compensation for

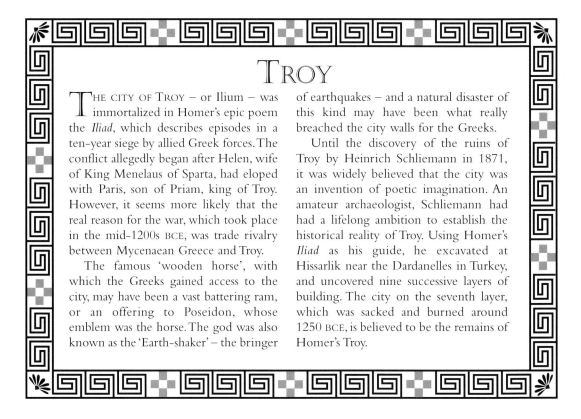

TROY

THE CITY OF TROY – or Ilium – was immortalized in Homer's epic poem the *Iliad*, which describes episodes in a ten-year siege by allied Greek forces. The conflict allegedly began after Helen, wife of King Menelaus of Sparta, had eloped with Paris, son of Priam, king of Troy. However, it seems more likely that the real reason for the war, which took place in the mid-1200s BCE, was trade rivalry between Mycenaean Greece and Troy.

The famous 'wooden horse', with which the Greeks gained access to the city, may have been a vast battering ram, or an offering to Poseidon, whose emblem was the horse. The god was also known as the 'Earth-shaker' – the bringer

of earthquakes – and a natural disaster of this kind may have been what really breached the city walls for the Greeks.

Until the discovery of the ruins of Troy by Heinrich Schliemann in 1871, it was widely believed that the city was an invention of poetic imagination. An amateur archaeologist, Schliemann had had a lifelong ambition to establish the historical reality of Troy. Using Homer's *Iliad* as his guide, he excavated at Hissarlik near the Dardanelles in Turkey, and uncovered nine successive layers of building. The city on the seventh layer, which was sacked and burned around 1250 BCE, is believed to be the remains of Homer's Troy.

his loss, Agamemnon took Briseis from Achilles. Enraged at this injustice, Achilles withdrew from the field of battle, taking all his Myrmidon warriors with him and leaving Agamemnon to soldier on as best he might.

Seeing the departure of Achilles, the Trojans seized their chance and made a vigorous attack. With his forces so depleted, Agamemnon was afraid and offered a truce.

'This quarrel is not between us,' he said. 'It is between two men – let them fight in single combat to settle this dispute.'

And so it was that Paris and Menelaus faced each other in a duel to decide the fate of Helen and of Troy. But seeing Paris stagger beneath the assault of Menelaus, Aphrodite – ever-watchful of her protégé – enfolded him in an enchanted mist and carried him back into Troy.

Next to duel were the mighty Ajax and Hector, son of Priam, leader of the Trojans and as brave and true a man as ever walked the earth. All day the pair were locked in combat, shield hitting shield and blade meeting blade until at last, as a slow sun slid behind the western horizon suffusing the sky with fire, all agreed that the pair were so evenly matched that neither – and both – had won. It was then, in one of those unexpected gestures of war when a man perceives in his enemy a shared and noble humanity, that the two adversaries exchanged gifts in recognition of each other's courage. Hector gave Ajax his silver-studded sword; Ajax gave Hector his purple baldric, his warrior's belt.

This duel, however, had been as inconclusive as the last, and when the truce was lifted and fighting resumed, the Trojans, aided by Zeus, drove the Greeks back to their ships.

And still proud Achilles sat, brooding on injustice and refusing to join the battle.

Agamemnon was desperate. He sent messengers to Achilles with offers of placatory gifts.

'Tell him I will give him silver! And gold! And horses! And slaves! Tell him I will give him Briseis, and that she is still a virgin.'

But still Achilles was proud and would not forgive Agamemnon.

All this time, high up on lofty Olympus, Hera had been watching the conflict. She had never forgotten how Paris had slighted her and had vowed revenge on him and all his kin. It was time, she decided, to turn the tide of the Trojans' success. To distract Zeus' attention from the action, she persuaded Aphrodite to let her borrow her magic girdle. Adorned in this, she would be irrestible to her husband, and while he was otherwise occupied, the sea-god Poseidon would be able to rally the ship-bound Greeks and rout the Trojans.

All happened as Hera had planned, but she could not detain Zeus forever, however pleasurable the reason. When he saw what had been happening while his back was turned, he ordered Poseidon to go back where he belonged, to the sea.

When the fighting resumed anew, it was the Trojans who gained the upper hand, and many of the Greeks were wounded, Agamemnon and Odysseus among them.

And still proud Achilles withheld his help, even threatening to leave Troy altogether and return home to Thessaly.

THE WRATH OF ACHILLES

At last, Patroclus went to Achilles to explain the dire state in which the Greeks found themselves, and to appeal to him – in the name of their friendship – to come to the aid of his comrades.

Achilles listened carefully to what Patroclus had to say, and then replied:

'It grieves me greatly to hear your words, dear friend, and I weep for the Greek dead and wounded. But great disrespect has been paid me, and the apologies of Agamemnon pour as easy from his lips as water from a sieve. No, I will not rejoin the field, but there is another way – you, Patroclus, must go in my stead. You must lead the Myrmidons for me.'

And so it was that Achilles put his own armour on the back of Patroclus and sent him – his dearest friend and boyhood companion – out into the forefront of battle.

A mighty roar went up amongst the Greeks when they saw a figure they took to be the returned Achilles, with his Myrmidons, hurl himself into the thick of the fighting; and panic struck the hearts of the Trojans as they tried to escape. It was now that Hector, leaping from his chariot to defend his charioteer, came face to face with Patroclus. With Apollo by his side, guiding his hand, Hector ran his spear deep into the heart of his foe, and killed him. Then he removed his own armour, took that of Patroclus, and put it on.

While the Greeks tried to gain possession of the body of the slain hero – for it was important that it be properly honoured with the sacred funeral rites – a messenger was sent to Achilles to tell him of the death of his friend.

The howl that arose from the throat of Achilles was like that of a wounded animal, dying and in pain. No, it could not be! Not his friend, who had been to him like an older brother, advising him, guiding him, just as their fathers had wished when the two were boys. No, not Patroclus, companion of all his days! It was unbearable, for was it not he himself who, through his obstinate pride, had sent his friend to his death?

A kind of madness descended on Achilles, and so loud was his wailing that it even alerted his mother Thetis, deep in her home under the sea, and she came to investigate. Bloody revenge, her son told her, was the only cure for his pain. Thetis, however, counselled patience at least, that is, until she had time to have new armour made for him by Hephaestus, blacksmith to the gods. A day later, the armour was ready and Achilles put it on. He then made peace with Agamemnon, and prepared to avenge the death of his friend.

Fired with a wild battle-frenzy, his strength was that of fifty men. He gave no quarter and showed no mercy. None could withstand his wrath, as he scythed through the enemy ranks, slashing, slicing, severing, chopping, hacking, and sending the terrified Trojans fleeing for their lives. At last, Achilles came upon his quarry, the man whose death was the only solace he sought: Hector, the murderer of his friend.

As the two came face to face, a terrible silence fell and warriors on both sides, who only seconds before had been engaged in bloody combat, let their weapons fall and looked on in fascination and horror. As Hector stood there, preparing to meet whatever destiny intended for him, the words of his wife Andromache floated into his mind.

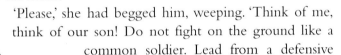

'Please,' she had begged him, weeping. 'Think of me, think of our son! Do not fight on the ground like a common soldier. Lead from a defensive position, where you will be safer.'

But that was something Hector could not do, for his hero's code of valour prevented him. He could not allow his men to fight and die, while he stood aloof. The city and all its people depended on him. Did not his very name – Hector – mean 'Holder'? As long as he was able, he would do whatever he could to protect Troy, even though, deep in the marrow of his bones, he felt his cause was hopeless.

And now here he stood before the greatest warrior in all of Greece, who lusted for his death. The pair set to, thrusting swords and locking shields, watched by a crowd frozen in hushed expectancy. Then Hector did an extraordinary thing. Perhaps he thought to tire Achilles, so long inactive; or perhaps it was simply that even his great heart failed him. Hector turned on his heel and ran. Following the great wall that circled the city, Achilles pursued his opponent, staying with him over stones and ditches, over earth and scrub. Three times they made the circuit around Troy, and each time Hector tried to enter one of the city gates where his brothers were waiting, Achilles was there first, blocking his path.

At last, Hector could run no more. He stopped, stood his ground, and prepared to face his death. And Achilles, with all the practised deftness of the seasoned warrior that he was, ran Hector through the breast with his sword. As the Trojan lay dying, he made a last plea.

'My body …' he whispered, 'let my body be ransomed for burial.'

But Achilles refused. With the madness still on him, he slit the tendons of Hector's heels, and threaded through them the baldric given by Ajax, which Hector still wore. Then he tied the baldric to his chariot, whipped up his horses, and dragged the body of the Trojan hero around the walls of the city – once, twice, three times – while up in the towers of Troy Hecabe, the victim's mother, Priam, his father, and Andromache, his wife, looked on, helpless and in horror, at this cruelty played out before them.

Achilles then ordered a great pyre built for the funeral of Patroclus, his friend. Wood was collected from Mount Ida and horses, hounds, and Trojan prisoners – sons of Priam among them – were sacrificed in the flames. Achilles would have thrown Hector's body onto the pyre, too, but Aphrodite stopped him.

His mind still infected with madness, Achilles kept the body of his enemy by him, and every day at dawn dragged it three times around the grave of Patroclus. Bumping and bobbing over sticks and stones and rocks, the corpse would have been torn and mutilated had not Apollo protected it, keeping Hector as fair in death as he had been in life.

At last, under cover of night, Hermes – god of travellers and soul-guide – brought Priam to Achilles to beg for the release of his son's body, in return for its weight in gold.

'Think, my son, of your own father,' Priam reminded him. 'Would he not wish for you a hero's farewell?'

Pity finally softened the hard heart of Achilles, and he consented.

Scales were set up outside the city walls, and Hector's great bulk placed in one pan. But no matter how much of Troy's fabled wealth was piled in the other, the scales were still imbalanced. Priam's coffers had been all but emptied, when the king's daughter Polyxena, who had been watching the weighing, removed all her gold bracelets and threw them down, tipping the scales just enough to bring them into perfect balance. This act of selflessness did not go unnoticed by Achilles.

'I will have that woman to my wife,' he thought.

The Trojans then took the body of Hector into Troy for the funeral rites. Nine days was the pyre in the making, and when the torch was put to it and the fire had done its work, the bones of Hector were placed in a golden urn and buried in the earth. And so Ilium honoured the passing of her greatest hero, and they say that so great was the wailing of the people that the birds of the air, stunned, fell from the sky.

Achilles' end, too, would not be long in coming. Some say that he was killed on the field of battle; others, that he was murdered while negotiating peace with the Trojans in return for Polyxena. All, however, agree on the identity of his assailant. It was Paris – his hand guided by Apollo, his aim unerring – who shot his arrow at the one spot on Achilles' entire body that was not protected by immortality: his heel. As Achilles lay dying, the last word he spoke was 'Polyxena'.

Ajax and Odysseus rescued the body of the hero. Thetis, accompanied by sea-nymphs, came to grieve for her son, and the Muses sang his soul on its way to everlasting life. For seventeen days and nights the mourning continued, and then the body of Achilles was offered up on the pyre and his ashes, mixed with those of Patroclus, buried in a golden urn made by Hephaestos, the god who had made his armour.

Thetis wished to bequeath the armour to the most courageous of the Greeks still left alive. There could only be two contenders: Ajax and Odysseus. At last, after much deliberating, Odysseus was chosen, whereupon Ajax, incensed at this slight to his valour, plotted to revenge himself on his fellow Greeks. But here Athene intervened and replaced the murder in his mind with madness.

That night, raging amongst the cattle and sheep taken from the Trojans, Ajax indulged in an orgy of slaughter, even believing two of the rams to be Agamemnon and Odysseus and abusing them accordingly. But as a dove-grey dawn lit the sky, he came to his senses and his madness was replaced by despair. He took his sword – the one which, only hours before, had been the agent of so much butchery, the one given him by Hector – and, placing it under his arm, drove his body down onto it until it pierced it through.

Later, in the place where his blood had pooled, a small flower sprouted. It was the hyacinth, and in the shape of its leaves two Greek letters could be deciphered: 'ai', the first two letters of the name 'Ajax' – 'ai', the Greek word for 'woe'.

THE DEATH OF PARIS

So much carnage, so much waste, so many dead, the bravest and the best. Nine years had passed since the Greeks set sail for Troy, and now, in the tenth year of the siege, the city still held out, Helen still lingered within. Other strategems would have to be employed if the Greeks were to take Troy.

A prophecy was then recalled, that the city could only be taken with the aid of the deadly arrows of Heracles. These were now in the possession of Philoctetes, one of the Greek expedition and the man who had lighted the pyre of the dying Heracles and had received the arrows in thanks. Philoctetes was duly summoned, and almost immediately challenged Paris to a duel, to which Paris agreed.

Raising his bow, the Greek fired off his first arrow. It went wide of its mark. The second disabled the bow-hand of the Trojan. The third blinded him in the eye. The fourth pierced his ankle and sent its poison into his veins.

Knowing that he was mortally wounded, Paris sent for the river-nymph Oenone whom he had loved all those years ago – in another lifetime, it seemed, before he had first set eyes on Helen, before the world had begun to crumble. She alone, he knew, would be able to cure him with her healing herbs. But Oenone, whom he had deserted in favour of Helen, refused his plea. And when at last, relenting, she hurried down from the mountains with her basket of herbs, she found Paris dead, his face turned to the wall.

THE WOODEN HORSE

The demise of Paris, however, did nothing to further the Greek cause. It was then that another prophecy was remembered: Troy would never fall as long as the statue of Athene known as the Palladium – a sacred image said to have fallen from heaven – remained within its walls. Crafty Odysseus, disguised as a runaway slave, gained entry to the city and made the necessary theft. Yet still Ilium continued to elude the Greeks, still her ramparts reared their impenetrable flanks, unassailable.

The ruse that finally caused the towers of Troy to tumble had more to do with perfidious tactics than with prophecies and magic. It was an idea that would be credited to the cunning of Odysseus.

Burning their camp, the Greeks made a great show of preparing to abandon the siege. Then they took their ships and put out to sea, as if sailing away for good. In reality, they anchored off some neighbouring islands, and waited.

Meanwhile, the Trojans, believing that their enemy had finally gone, gave up a mighty cheer, flung open the gates of the city, and came pouring down onto the shore. And there before them, surrounded by the smouldering remains of the Greek camp, loomed – a horse! A vast, sky-scraping, wooden horse. The Trojans examined it, and saw, inscribed in large letters on its side, a dedication to Athene. It was an offering from the Greeks to the goddess of war, asking her to send them a safe and speedy return home. The enemy had truly left! The horse was a gift that signalled peace.

The Trojans were delighted, and wanted to bring the wonderful trophy into the city at once. But Laocoön, a priest of Poseidon who was among them, was wary. Suspecting treachery, he tried to dissuade his fellow Trojans.

'It is a trick – do not be taken in by it!' he cried. 'Fear the Greeks when they come bearing gifts!' And he threw his lance at the horse's side.

Just then, some soldiers arrived, dragging with them a Greek prisoner. His name was Sinon, the prisoner said, and he had escaped from his comrades who had been planning to give him in sacrifice to the gods. When questioned about the wooden horse, Sinon confirmed that it was indeed an offering to Athene.

'But why its great size?' asked Priam.

'That, sire,' replied Sinon, 'is to prevent you bringing it into Troy. For if you do, you will become unconquerable and will vanquish all of Greece.'

While the argument raged over the fate of the horse a terrible portent was seen. As a sign that Troy was doomed, Apollo sent two serpents across the sea. They came slithering across the sands, wrapped themselves around Laocoön and his two sons, and crushed them to death.

The crowd, however, took this as an indication of divine anger at the priest. And so they hauled the great horse into the city, garlanding its mane with flowers and throwing rose petals before its hooves. Oh, and what merry-making there was in Ilium that night! How the wine flowed; how the banquet tables groaned; how the laughter rang out as the Trojans, free at last, celebrated their victory. Surfeited with happiness, they finally went to their beds to enjoy the deepest sleep they had had in ten years.

Out in the Trojan night, the wooden effigy still stood, its flanks silvered by moonlight. The light also caught on a small trap-door, almost invisibly fitted into one side. When he judged that the whole city was lost to sleep, Sinon crept out and opened the door and out from their hiding place in the horse's capacious belly they came – Odysseus, Menelaus, Diomedes, Thoas, Acamus, and many, many more. The signal was given from a turret to the waiting ships out at anchor, the city gates were flung open, and the Greek army entered and swarmed over Troy like ants from a broken nest, killing as they went. The old, the young, the healthy, the infirm, slaughtered in their beds as they slept! Few were spared. Aged Priam was murdered on the steps of his palace. His daughter Cassandra was seized as Agamemnon's prize – but not before she had been violated by the altar of Athene, causing the goddess's statue to turn its eyes to heaven in horror. Polyxena was sacrificed on the grave of Achilles. Hecabe was given to Odysseus. Andromache was taken by Neoptolemus and her infant son by Hector hurled to his death from the battlements.

When at last the killing stopped, the Greeks torched the city and razed it to the ground, columns of smoke drifting heavenward to mingle with the clouds. Out of the death of this city came the birth of another, for Aeneas, son-in-law to Priam and fugitive from Troy, would later settle on the banks of the Tiber to become the founder of Rome

As for Helen, whose folly had been the cause of so much destruction, she had long ago regretted it and when Menelaus found her, she was relieved to go with him. In the years to come, a rumour would grew that she had never been in Troy at all, and that what Paris brought back was merely a phantom made of mist while the real Helen waited in Egypt. But perhaps this was just a fiction invented to preserve the esteem of Menelaus.

What of the other Greeks? Achilles and Ajax were dead, and Odysseus was cursed to wander the seas for another ten years before he could arrive, destitute and unrecognizable, on the shores of Ithaca once more. Agamemnon did return home, to his wife Clytemnestra, Helen's sister. But Clytemnestra had never forgiven him for the death – or disappearance – of their daughter Iphigenia. While Agamemnon was in his bath, she and her lover murdered him, imprisoning him in a net, stabbing him, and beheading him.

Later, the murder would be avenged by Orestes, son of Agamemnon and Clytemnestra, who would kill his mother and his mother's lover, and would in consequence be plagued by the black Furies, those winged spirits of conscience, until driven beyond the boundary that divides reason from madness.

But all of that is, as they say, another story …

THE WANDERINGS OF ODYSSEUS

One day, on the island of Scheria where the Phaecians dwell, a princess and her handmaids had come to wash the princess's royal robes in the river that runs strong and clear, between banks of clover and olives, down to the wine-dark sea. After cooling themselves in the crystal waters, they oiled their skins and laid their clothes on the rocks to dry; they ate

the picnic of savouries and sweetmeats prepared for them, and drank a skin of wine; and now they were playing ball.

Round the circle the ball went until at last, slipping through the fingers of one of the girls, it landed with a splash in the swirling stream. The princess and her handmaids gave out a great cry … and deep in the undergrowth something stirred.

As they watched in trepidation, the branches of the olive trees shook and parted and out came a man, magnificent as a mountain lion but naked as a newborn babe except for the olive branch which he held to cover himself. His hair and beard were matted, his skin crusted with the salt of the sea.

The handmaids fled in panic but the princess, summoning all the courage that flowed in her royal veins, stood her ground as the stranger approached her and threw himself on her mercy. So honeyed were his words that the fear she had felt was replaced with pity. She gave the stranger a cloak to cover his nakedness, seated him in her wagon, and drove him to the palace in which she lived, for she was the white-armed Princess Nausicaa, daughter of Alcinoüs, king of the Phaecians.

THE SONG OF THE BARD

In the golden halls of the palace, surrounded on all sides by broad and abundant orchards, the king welcomed the stranger whom his daughter had discovered. But some deep sorrow seemed to occupy the stranger's mind for he sat apart from the company, huddling by the ashes of the fire. This was no fit way to welcome a guest and the king insisted that he came and sat by his side in a burnished chair. He ordered food and wine brought, and was glad to see his guest eat and drink his fill.

The following day, when the company were again banqueting, Demodocus, the blind bard, came to entertain them.

'Sing to us, Demodocus,' said the king. 'Sing us songs of heroes, tell us tales of valour, fill us with the glory of battles long ago.'

And the bard picked up his lyre and began. He sang of the city of Troy and of Helen, stolen by Paris, prince of Troy; he sang of the thousand ships that crossed the sea to bring her back. He sang of the heroes who had died – of Patroclus and Hector; of Achilles, shot in his vulnerable heel; of Ajax, pierced by the point of his own sword; of Agamemnon, murdered by his wife. He sang, too, of Odysseus, who had never returned home and was presumed lost at sea.

The beauty and sadness of his song touched the hearts of all who heard it, but they seemed especially to touch the heart of the stranger who sat with tears coursing unchecked down his cheeks.

The king was greatly concerned. 'Dear friend,' he enquired, 'does the song distress you? Perhaps one of your own acquaintance died by the walls of Troy – a comrade, or a blood-brother? Tell us, stranger … tell us who you are.'

'I,' replied the stranger, 'am that Odysseus of whom the bard sings. Ten years was I at

Troy, and nine full years have passed since I left there, all as the oracle foretold. Doomed to twenty years of exile if I went to fight the Trojans, I used all my cunning to avoid the call. I feigned madness – yoking an ox and an ass together and throwing salt over my shoulder as I ploughed. But my deceit was uncovered when they placed my infant son Telemachus in my path. Sailing with the hollow ships, I left behind my wife Penelope and my beloved island of Ithaca. I have wandered the seas and faced dangers of every imaginable kind. You see me here now, a king without a crown, a captain without a crew, a shipwrecked mariner with no means – or hope – of ever going home.'

Greatly moved by these words, Alcinoüs spoke. 'Let not such sorrow consume your soul. I will provide you with a vessel. I will give you a crew – and provisions, too, for your voyage back to Ithaca. But first, noble king, honour us with your story. Tell us of all the adventures that befell you on the broad back of the sea.'

And so Odysseus began his tale.

THE LOTUS-EATERS

'With twelve ships at my command I left Troy, by now a smouldering ruin. I sailed westward to Thrace and, coming upon the city of Ismarus, attacked and plundered it, losing six men from each of my ships in the fighting.

'I then put out to sea again, taking a southerly course, but angry Zeus sent a gale that blew us off course, driving us helplessly hither and thither for nine full days and nights.

'At last, on the tenth day, the gale ceased and we sighted land. I sent a scouting party of three men ashore. Had I known what awaited them I would have kept them on board and set sail at once, for we had come to the Land of the Lotus-eaters. The inhabitants of this place feed on an enchanted fruit which erases all memories of home and family, and leaves the eater sapped of his will.

'When my men did not return, I was then forced to go in search of them, and found the fools reclining at their ease as if they had not a care in the world, like men who are drunk on wine. Resisting all offers of the magic berries, I dragged the deserters back to the ships, bound them fast to the rowing benches, and set my course once more.'

'Such bold resolve takes the greatest courage,' remarked King Alcinoüs. 'But tell us – what danger befell you next?'

Odysseus resumed his tale.

THE ONE-EYED GIANT

'Our next port-of-call was a fertile, well-wooded island. Leaving the main body of my ships at anchor, I landed with twelve of my men, bringing with us a skin of wine as a gift. We saw no one, but came at last upon a vast cavern in the rocky hills, with laurels growing around its mouth. Inside we found an orderly scene. On large, flat racks cheeses were drying; there were pails and buckets brimming with whey; and in stone enclosures lambs and kids frolicked.

'While we awaited the return of the cave's owner, we made a feast of the food that was

there. At last, as evening drew near, our unwitting host returned, driving before him the flocks which he had pastured during the day. You can imagine our horror, dear king, when we saw that the person whose hospitality we had enjoyed was a Cyclops – a creature as tall as a tree with only one eye in the middle of his forehead. His name, as I later discovered, was Polyphemus, and he was the son of the sea-god Poseidon.

'Polyphemus threw down the bundle of firewood he was carrying and, when the flock was safely inside, sealed up the entrance to the cave with a boulder so vast that twenty wagons could not have shifted it. Then he squatted down to milk his animals, setting half the milk aside for curdling and pressing, the other half to drink. It was then that his great eye slewed around the interior, and settled on us!

'Knowing that our lives depended on it, I explained as humbly as I could that we were Greek heroes returning from Troy, and asked his hospitality in the name of the gods. "What care I, Polyphemus, for Greek heroes?" he scoffed. "The flesh of one tastes as good

143

as another!" And so saying, he seized two of my men, dashed their brains out on the cave wall, and devoured them for his supper.

'The following morning, as rosy-fingered Dawn lit the sky, the Cyclops selected two more of my men for a light breakfast. Then he drove his cattle out to pasture as before, taking care to seal the cave behind him.

'With nothing to do but wait for the ogre's return, I examined the cave and spied, on the floor, a great olive-wood stave intended by the giant for his new club. This gave me an idea. I told my companions to smooth the sides of the stave, while I whittled away the tip to a point as sharp as a spear.

'That evening, after two more men had gone the way of their comrades, I put my plan into action. Producing the wine skin I had brought from the ships, I offered the Cyclops a bowl of the honeyed juice – "It is the perfect complement to a meal of human flesh," I said.

'Clearly, the Cyclops had never drunk anything stronger than buttermilk before, and the wine went straight to his head. He demanded another bowlful, which I readily supplied, and then another and another.

'The wine worked its alchemy to ease the giant's temper, and in a slurred but friendly voice he asked, "What is thy name, thou minute morsel, thou puny mouthful? Who art thou?"

'"I am Nobody," I replied.

'"Well, Nobody, in return for thy wondrous potion, I mean to favour thee greatly – I shall eat thee last!" And so saying, he fell to the floor, blind-drunk.

'Instantly, my men and I seized the stave we had prepared and held it in the fire until it was red-hot as a burning coal. Then we plunged it into the giant's sleeping eye, turning it round and round in the broiling, sizzling, spurting socket like an auger boring into wood.

'Hearing the roars of Polyphemus as we put out his eye, all his fellows from round about came to see what might be the matter. "Who hath hurt thee?" they called. "Nobody!" "Well, if nobody has caused thy pain, nobody is to blame," and with these words, they went on their way.

'Next morning, when rosy-fingered Dawn brought the light and Polyphemus was preparing to roll the boulder from the door once more, I had his rams harnessed three abreast. Clinging to the belly of the middle ram, one man to every threesome, we escaped the giant's attention as he felt for us with his blind-man's fingers, and so passed safely out with the flock.'

'A cunning escape indeed!' said King Alcinoüs. 'But where did you direct yourself next?'

Odysseus continued his story.

THE LORD OF THE WINDS

'Adopting a northerly course, we arrived in time at the island of King Aeolus. This, as you may have heard tell, is an isle unlike any other for it floats with the sea-tides at the whim of the waves. Here Aeolus lives contentedly with his twelve sons and twelve daughters, and sends forth or calls in the winds which have been placed in his charge by Zeus.

'Aeolus received me most hospitably and entertained me and my companions lavishly for a full month. Then, as a parting gift from host to guest, he gave me a leather sack tied with a silver cord, in which he had imprisoned all the gales and other breezes so they would not trouble our course, leaving free only Zephyrus the West Wind to waft us over the sea to Ithaca. "Take care not to open the sack," he warned me, "until thou art home on the shores of Ithaca, or it will go the worse for thee," and so saying, he bade us a courteous farewell.

'For nine days and nine nights we sailed, and not once in all that time did I sleep for I feared that my men, believing the sack to contain gold or wine, would open it. At last, when we were so close to home that I could see the smoke rising from the hearths of my palace, I felt that the danger was past and succumbed to Sleep, who closes all men's eyes in sweet rest. No sooner had I done so, however, than my men, in their greed, tore open the sack. The winds, jubilant to be free, roared about in gleeful abandon and tore off in the direction of their home, bearing us before them from Ithaca back to the island of Aeolus.

'This time, the king's welcome was not so warm. He refused us even a light breeze to ruffle our sails, and we were forced to make our own way by rowing with our oars.'

'Is it not man's lot ...' the king reflected, 'to be in reach of his heart's desire, only to see it snatched from beneath his watching eyes?'

Odysseus returned to his tale.

THE ISLAND OF CANNIBALS

'After a voyage of seven days, we came to the island of the Laestrygones, giants who feed on human flesh. In this place, Dawn follows so closely on the heels of Night that those driving their flocks home in the evening meet those driving them out in the morning.

'While the captains of my other ships boldly entered the harbour, I – being more wary – remained at anchor outside. My fears proved well-founded when one of the three scouts I had sent inland was killed and prepared for the pot. The other two fled for their lives. Their appetites whetted, the Laestrygones made for the cliffs above the harbour and pelted the ships below with a hail of rocks, smashing them to pieces. With no means of escape, the terrified sailors provided an easy meal. The giants picked them out of the water and devoured them at their leisure. Only I and the companions on my ship escaped this hideous fate.'

'Your instincts served you well,' observed the king, 'or you, too, would have been cannibal's fare.'

Odysseus continued his tale.

THE DAUGHTER OF THE SUN

'Glad to have preserved our lives but grieving for our dead comrades, we sailed eastwards and presently arrived at Aeaea, the Island of the Dawn. I sent a party ashore, led by my comrade Eurylochus, to see what might be found. Passing through thick forests, they came at last to a clearing in the midst of which stood a magnificent palace. All around it prowled lions and wolves, but instead of attacking the visitors they approached them and nuzzled and pawed them in the most affectionate manner, like hounds greeting their master.

'Coming from inside the palace, the party then heard the sound of the sweetest singing. On peering inside, they saw a woman, beautiful as a goddess, plying back and forth on a loom and weaving a web of such fineness as only the Immortals can. This, it transpired, was Circe, Daughter of the Sun.

'She invited the visitors in and all entered save Eurylochus who, suspecting a trap, waited and watched from outside. Circe then laid a meal before her guests – a concoction of cheese, barley, honey and wine. Little knowing that the brew was drugged, the innocents drained their bowls and instantly lost all memory of who they were, where they had come from, and where they were going. The enchantress then tapped each lightly on the shoulder and where a man had stood, there now stood a hog! She then drove the hapless creatures into a sty, threw a few acorns before them, and left them to wallow in silent misery.

'All this I know because Eurylochus relayed it to me on his return, weeping at what he had witnessed. I at once seized my sword and made off for the palace of Circe, but on the path I was waylaid by a youth who introduced himself to me as the god Hermes. Aware of the plight of my fellows, he gave me a magic herb to protect me against the spells of witches. It is called Moly, and only the gods know where to cull it.

'The sorceress welcomed me with every courtesy, and gave me the same meal as she had given my companions. But when she touched me on the shoulder, her wand was powerless to harm me for I had breathed in the perfume of the magic herb. I raised my sword to strike her, but she fell swooning at my feet and begged for mercy. "Spare my life," she pleaded, "and thou mayest share my bed and rule by my side as my king."

'Now I have to admit that her offer was tempting for she was fair beyond words. But knowing the power of witches, how they entice men with their advances only to drain them of their lives, I declined. Instead, I made her swear by the gods that she would do me no mischief, and further insisted that she un-charm not only my comrades but also all those other seafarers held under her spell.

'That done, I was able to accept her invitation and proceeded to enjoy the considerable pleasures that she had to offer. Days, nights, and whole seasons passed in this delightful manner until a year had gone by without my noticing. I might be with Circe still had not my loyal companions pointed out my folly. "Master," they said, "it is time to go home."

'I knew then that I must leave and – with the greatest reluctance – prepared to depart.'

'And thereby escaped Oblivion,' added King Alcinoüs, 'which comes in many forms.'

Odysseus resumed his account.

THE LAND OF THE DEAD

'Having enlisted Circe's help in making the voyage home, she advised me to go to Tartarus, the Land of the Dead, that lies across the Ocean. There, she said, I should seek out the blind seer Teiresias, who would be able to forewarn me of what I could expect on my journey.

'I was horror-struck at her words. "No ship can sail to the Land of the Dead," I protested, "and still less a man return from there."

'But Circe calmed my fears. "Go before the North Wind," she said. "Boreas will carry you there." And so, with great misgivings, I set off.

'All happened as the enchantress predicted, and at last I found myself on the shores of Death, and arrived at Persephone's Grove. There I made the offerings to the dead as Circe had instructed: the first of milk and honey; the second of wine; the third of water; and I sprinkled all with barley. Finally, I slaughtered a ram and a black ewe and let the blood collect in a trench. All at once, a great swarm of Shades – the spirits of the dead – gathered around me, eager to drink the blood. Even my own mother was amongst them, but I held them all back for I knew that the first sip belonged to Teiresias.

'At last he appeared, the Shade of the Prophet of Thebes. Having lapped at the blood, he then told me my future.

'"Thy voyage home shall be a perilous one, and thou might yet achieve the shores of Ithaca – but it will be as a man alone, wretched and unknown. Thou willst find thy wife besieged by scoundrels who would usurp thy place. All this thou willst overcome and live to enjoy a ripe old age; and when at last Death comes for thee, it will come from the sea."

'Thanking Teiresias, I made my farewells to the Shades of friends long dead – Achilles, Agamemnon, and Ajax from Troy among them. Then, returning by the same way as I had come, I arrived back at the Island of the Dawn.'

'To sail to the shores of Death – that, surely, was your greatest challenge!' said the king.

Odysseus went on with his story.

THE SIRENS

'Back at the Island, Circe the Sun's Daughter greeted me warmly. "One death suffices most men," she said, laughing, "but thou, returned from the dead, hast two!" She then warned me of certain dangers I would face on my outward voyage, and advised me as to how I might circumvent them. Thanking her, I set sail, and my ship was carried along by a fair breeze.

'Presently my companions and I encountered the first hazard of which the enchantress had spoken. This was the island of the Sirens, creatures with the faces of women but the bodies of birds. The allure of these flightless temptresses lies in their singing voices, which are so ravishingly beautiful that sailors will fling themselves overboard to come closer to them, only to be dashed to their death on the rocks. If we were not to add ourselves to the victims whose bones now littered the shore, we had to guard ourselves against the Sirens's spell. Accordingly, as Circe had instructed, I ordered my men to stop up their ears with beeswax, and to lash me to the mast. Moreover, I said, they should not untie me no matter how hard I pleaded.

'As we came within range of the singing, I was in torment. I yearned with every fibre of my being to be free of my bonds for the song seemed to seep into my very soul, and I wished to drown myself in it. I strained at the mast but my comrades, heeding my instructions, tightened my bonds still further and refused to release me until we were safely out of temptation.'

'Had you not resisted those seductresses,' said the king, 'the waves might be washing your bones even now.'

Odysseus resumed his story.

THE MONSTROUS CLIFFS

'We continued on our way and shortly came to the second hazard of which Circe had spoken – the two dreaded cliffs. On one cliff dwells a monster by the name of Scylla. Long ago, she was a beautiful maiden but was transformed by a jealous goddess into a monster with six heads and twelve feet. Now, on her clifftop lookout, she watches for approaching ships and picks off the sailors from the decks as they sail by, crunching their bones and eating them.

'At the foot of the facing cliff – barely more than a ship's width across – lies Charybdis. This monster is like a vast, voracious mouth, who three times a day sucks in a great volume of water, and then regurgitates it again.

'There was no way forward for my ship other than between these two terrors. As captain, I knew that our only hope was to steer an exact course down the middle of the channel. But in seeking to avoid Charybdis, I sailed too near Scylla who snatched six of my men from the deck, one for each of her mouths, and bore them off to devour them. As she carried them aloft, they reached out their arms to me and cried out to me to save them, but I dared not or we should all perish. The sight of their faces and the sound of their screams is something that will haunt me until my dying day.'

'You could not have done otherwise,' said the king, 'or you yourself might have suffered the same fate.'

Odysseus picked up the thread of his story.

THE CATTLE OF THE SUN

'I sailed on and after some time arrived at Thrinakia, the Island of the Sun. On this isle lives the god Helios. Here he keeps seven herds of magnificent cattle, and several flocks as well. Each day, when rosy-fingered Dawn comes to wake him, the god seats himself in his golden winged boat and sails across the sky, driving his cattle before him.

'Teiresias the prophet had warned me that it would bring sure disaster if we so much as touched the cattle of the Sun, and I made my men swear on oath that they would not steal even a single cow. We had, in any event, sufficient provisions on board to sustain us, so there was no need for my companions to take what was not theirs.

'Unluckily our stay on the island was extended, for Eurus the South Wind blew day and night for a full month and prevented our departure. In the end, all our store of food was gone and we were forced to eke a meagre diet with such fish, birds and small animals as we could hunt or fish for ourselves. But what we were able to take in this way was barely enough to keep bone and sinew together, and starvation stared us in the face.

'At last, unable to bear any longer the hunger that gnawed at their bellies, my men waited until I was asleep. Then they caught and slaughtered several fat cows from the Sun's herds, promising to compensate Helios by erecting a temple to him on Ithaca on their return. They offered the gods their portion of the kill, and still had enough roasted meat left to feast for six days.

'I awoke and was horrified to see what they had done. I was even more afraid when they reported to me the omens they had seen. When they skinned the beasts, the hides had crept along the ground as if inhabited by spirits, and as the carcasses turned on the spit, they lowed as if still alive!

'Unable to undo the crime already done, I decided that our best course of action was to leave the island forthwith. By now, the wind had dropped sufficiently and the ship set sail, helped by a fair breeze.

'But all was not to remain calm, for Zeus the Sky Lord came to avenge my companions' crime by sending a violent storm. His thunderous anger shook the heavens and the lightning flash of his rage shattered the mast which fell, killing the helmsman. In the churning waves the ship foundered and sank, taking all on board with her, save me.

'His vengence accomplished, the Thunderer departed and I now found myself quite alone on the wide, wine-dark sea. The wreckage of my ship floated all around me. I seized the mast and bound it to the keel and so made myself a makeshift raft. On this I drifted I knew not whither, carried by the current for nine full days and nights.'

'A narrow escape!' said the king, 'You might otherwise have been at the sea-bottom, your flesh food for fishes.'

Odysseus returned to his story.

THE NYMPH CALYPSO

'At last, at the end of the ninth day, my craft was washed ashore on the island of Ogygia. Exhausted, I clambered to the top of a cliff where, gazing out across the blue waves, I wept for my friends, my wife, and my home.

'It was here that Calypso found me, the nymph of the lovely braids, sent to rescue me by the god Hermes. Taking me by the hand, she led me through thickets of alder, black poplar and cypress where owls, crows and falcons roost; past violet-starred meadows where sparkling brooks burble; and into the vine-garlanded entrance to a high-arched cavern, where a cedarwood fire burned, perfuming the air with its scent. Here, she gave me food to eat and heady wine to drink.

'"Why weepest thou for what is past?" she said. "Stay here with me and share my bed, and thou shalt live thy days in ease and pleasure and be one with the Immortals."

'What could I do? I had no ship to carry me away. I was a man alone in a hostile world. And so I resigned myself to my fate, and remained on Calypso's isle. By night I slept in her bed and allowed the enchantments of love to erase my sorrow. But by day, my memories would flood back. While the fair one sat singing by her loom, plying back and forth with a golden shuttle, I would return to the shore, and there I would sit, my body wracked with sobs.

'Seven years passed by in this fashion and Calypso would have retained me into eternity had not Zeus at last instructed her to release me. I was provided with materials to build a raft, and with corn, dried meat and wine for my voyage. After bidding the nymph farewell, I put out to sea, sped by a fair breeze. But worse was yet to come.

'As my raft drifted over the broad back of the sea, Poseidon the Wave-maker, returning from a visit to Ethiopia, spied me. You will remember, good king, that Poseidon was the father of Polyphemus, the Cyclops whom I had blinded at the start of my adventures.

'All the torments I had so far suffered were insufficient to assuage the god's anger at the wounding of his son. Alone on a raft in the middle of the sea, I was at his mercy, and he now vented on me all his rage. Lashing the sea to fury, he sent a huge wave crashing over me that swept me overboard. Plunged to the depths, I thought I might die, but managed with great effort to regain my raft – although I was now stripped of my robes. It was then that a small act of kindness saved my life. Leucothea, once a maiden but now transformed into a sea-bird, alighted on my raft. In her beak she carried a veil. "Tie this like a girdle around thy waist," she told me, "and it will bear thee across the waves. But as soon as thou art on dry land, return the girdle to the sea."

'Thanking her, I tied the magic girdle around my waist, and not a moment too soon for Poseidon churned the waters to a torrent of foam and broke the back of my raft, shattering it to pieces. I threw myself off it just in time and, buoyed by the girdle, swam and swam until at last I sank, exhausted, on the shores of your hospitable island. Having returned the girdle to the sea, I made myself a bed of leaves by a riverbank, and surrendered myself to sleep. It was there that your daughter Nausicaa found me. The rest you know.'

The mariner had finished his tale, and all sat speechless in awe at what they heard.

It was King Alcinoüs who broke the silence at last. 'Noble Odysseus, we thank you for your story, for you have told it well. But now, my friend, your tale is done, and it is time to return to Ithaca.'

And so saying, the good king furnished his guest with a fine vessel and crew to take him home. In the rear of the hollow ship, they laid out a linen sheet and a blanket on which he might lie, and as the vessel dipped and rose with the hypnotic swell of the sea, the weary mariner lowered himself onto his bed and Sleep, the twin of Death, claimed him.

And when Odysseus awoke he was in his native land, on the day when the New Moon meets the reborn Sun, the first day of the twentieth year.

HOMECOMING

'Where am I?' thought Odysseus, rubbing his eyes and looking about him, for Athene had shrouded the island in mist so that he did not know it.

'Thou art in Ithaca,' said the goddess, presently appearing to him. And Odysseus bent down and kissed the green earth and wept tears of joy.

Now while Odysseus had been away, affairs in his palace had gone from bad to worse. Believing him dead, no fewer than one hundred and twelve princes had come to court his wife Penelope, each hoping by marriage to take the throne for himself. Insolently, they had made themselves at home in the palace and refused to leave until the queen consented to choose one of them to be her new king.

Penelope, meanwhile, had remained faithful to her husband and sat every day weaving at her loom and awaiting his return. As to their son Telemachus, grown to manhood in his father's absence, he had never ceased searching for Odysseus and was now in Sparta, seeking news of him.

This, then, was the scene to which the king of Ithaca returned.

The task ahead, Athene told him, required cunning. He must go to it in disguise, unknown, a man with no name. And as she touched him lightly on the shoulder, he shrivelled in size, his smooth skin became lined and creased, his hair thinned, his royal robes ragged. He was, to all appearances, nothing but a wretched beggar, a Nobody.

The beggar-king proceeded to the hut of his swineherd Eumaeus, who had always been loyal to him, there to await Telemachus whom Athene was bringing back from Sparta. The goddess lifted Odysseus' disguise just long enough for Telemachus to recognize him, where-upon father and son threw their arms around each other and embraced, washing away their grief with the tears of twenty years.

Warning Telemachus to tell no one of his arrival, Odysseus set off for the palace to observe the suitors for himself. In the courtyard, he came upon his hunting dog, Argus. Now old, decrepit and mangy, the hound at once knew the beggar for who he truly was

HOMER AND HESIOD

HOMER IS THE most famous of the ancient Greek poets, but personal details of his life are obscure. His birth-dates have been placed between 1050 and 850 BCE, while Smyrna and Chios, as well as Rhodes, Colophon, Salamis, Argos and Athens, have all laid claim to being his birthplace. By tradition, he became poor and blind in his old age.

The epic poems the *Iliad* – describing the war between the Greeks and Trojans and probably composed between 725 and 675 BCE – and the *Odyssey* – describing the voyage of Odysseus and composed a little later – are both attributed to Homer. In the past, however, there has been controversy as to whether these were both the product of one mind, partly because of qualitative differences between them – the *Iliad* is heroic in tone, while the *Odyssey* deals in fable and displays a 'feminine' attention to domestic detail. It is not known whether Homer worked purely in the oral tradition of performance before an audience, and had his poems transcribed by someone else; or whether he took advantage of the new invention of writing to record them himself. Practical considerations (how could an illiterate poet compose and remember a piece so long that it took several days to perform, for example?) as well as a study of the verse itself suggest the latter.

Hesiod, another early Greek poet, may have lived and worked during the eighth century BCE. His origins were humble; born at Ascra in Boeotia, he became a shepherd, tending his father's flocks on Mount Helicon. According to tradition, he was eventually murdered at Oenoe in Locris.

His poems are *Works and Days*, which also describes country life in Boeotia; *Catalogue of Women*, which tells of women who have been loved by gods and have become the mothers of heroes; and the *Theogony*, an account of the mythical origins of the world and the genealogy of the Greek gods.

and wagged his ragged tail in greeting. At peace now that his master was home, the animal quietly expired where he lay.

Entering the palace hall, Odysseus went from one suitor to the next, humbly begging scraps from the table. But in each case he met with harsh words – 'Who are you, a nobody, to ask favours of the likes of us?' – and was roundly abused by the suitors.

Hearing that a stranger had arrived in the halls of Ithaca, and shocked at the treatment he had received, Penelope sent for the beggar in the hope that he might bear news of her long-lost husband. She told Eurycleia, Odysseus' old nurse, to bathe the guest's weary feet. As the aged dame was performing the task, she saw an unmistakable scar on his leg, the result of a wound Odysseus had received when gored by a boar.

'Master!' Eurycleia exclaimed in delight, but Odysseus hushed her to silence.

Telemachus then suggested to his mother a ruse whereby she might rid herself of the suitors for good.

'Set them a challenge,' he said. 'Tell them that you will only marry the man who can shoot an arrow from the bow of Odysseus through the rings of twelve axes.' The bow of which he spoke was an ancient one that now hung on the palace walls, and the feat was a favourite of Odysseus, which only he could do.

With much false boasting and bravado, the suitors arrived to demonstrate their prowess as archers. But not one of them could so much as bend the bow – even though they greased it with tallow – let alone shoot a single arrow through the line of axe-rings now set up before them.

'May I try my hand?' came a voice from the back of the hall. It was the ragged beggar.

'You? What does a wretch like you know of the skills of archery?' To the jeers and catcalls of the assembled princes Odysseus calmly raised his bow. It bent gracefully in recognition of his touch and he twanged the string like a minstrel plucking his lyre. Then he placed an arrow against it, drew back the bow and, with his steady eye fixed on his target, let fly. The dart winged through the air piercing one – two – three – six – nine – twelve rings in a single, swift, deft flight.

It was then that Penelope knew that her husband was home.

To make a long tale short, Odysseus and Telemachus, with the aid of the loyal swineherd and another faithful servant, despatched all the suitors while Athene, disguised as a sparrow, twittered overhead.

At last, Penelope was able to welcome Odysseus for whom she had been faithfully waiting for twenty years.

'Come, Sire, your bed is ready' she said. 'And later perhaps, when you are refreshed, you can tell me all the adventures you have had, out on the wine-dark sea.'

Reunited in each other's arms, husband and wife surrendered themselves up to joy until, replete with happiness, the wandering mariner began again his long tale.

The seasons wheeled by and the years came and went, bringing with them more adventures for Odysseus, who slowly grew into the fullness of old age. One day, hearing that Ithaca was under attack by a raiding party of ships, the renowned king sallied forth to the shore to repel the invaders. It was on the beach that he met their leader – Telegonus, his son by the enchantress Circe, who had come in search of his father and had mistaken the island for another. Not a flicker of recognition passed between the eyes of father and son.

The old king was swift, but Telegonus was swifter. Raising his spear, which he had tipped with the spine of a stingray, he plunged it deep into the breast of his unknown father. Sinking down onto the sand, Odysseus the Storm-tossed, Odysseus the Long-enduring breathed his last breath and was gently gathered up into the arms of Thanatos, who had been waiting for him on the beach all along.

So ends this tale of an ancient mariner, to whom Death came from the sea, just as the prophet had said it would, so long, long ago.

GLOSSARY AND NOTES

AEOLUS – Guardian of the Winds. The Aeolian Harp, whose strings emitted music when moved by the wind, was named after him.

APHRODITE – The Roman Venus, she was a pre-Olympian love-goddess. Her Asian counterparts were the Phoenician (Lebanese) Ashtaroth or Astarte, and the Babylonian Ishtar, whose young lover Tammuz, a sacrificial dying and reborn god, became Adonis in Greek tradition. She was the mother of Eros, either by Ares, Hephaestos or Hermes, and, by Anchises, the mother of Aeneas, said to be the founder of Rome.

APOLLO – Known by the same name to the Romans, he was thought to be of either Asiatic or Nordic origin. As the god of solar light (Helios represented the sun itself), he was also called Phoebus, 'the brilliant'. As well as his solar role, he was the Hellenic god of poetry and prophecy, and the brother of Artemis.

ARES – Known to the Romans as Mars, he was the god of war and lover or husband of Aphrodite.

ARTEMIS – The Roman Diana, she was the twin sister of Apollo. She was goddess of lunar light (Selene was goddess of the Moon), and of the hunt. In her great temple at Ephesus, she was worshipped as a many-breasted fertility goddess.

ATHENE – Also known as Athena, Pallas Athene, and the Roman Minerva, she was goddess of wisdom, war, and women's crafts. The olive tree, the owl and the spider belonged to her.

CERBERUS – The three-headed dog that guarded the entrance to Hades, kingdom of the dead. It was customary to place a cake in the hand of a dead person as a placatory gift to Cerberus to allow safe entrance into Hades, hence the phrase 'a sop to Cerberus'.

CHARON – The ferryman who ferried the dead over the River Styx. To pay him for this task, the Greeks would place a coin in the mouth or hand of the dead person, a token known as 'Charon's Toll'.

CRONOS – The Roman Saturn, he was one of the twelve Titans born to Gaia. His rule, which began after he castrated his father Ouranos, was a golden age. Banished by his son Zeus, he was exiled to the furthest edges of the earth where, on the Islands of the Blessed, his golden age continues.

DEMETER– The Roman Ceres, she was the goddess of the fruits of the earth, notably corn. As mother of Kore, later Persephone, she was the central figure of the Kore–Demeter–Persephone triad (maiden–mother–crone). The Eleusinian Mysteries were celebrated in her honour, and to commemorate the departure and return of Kore. The mare and sow were sacred to her.

DIONYSOS – The Roman Bacchus, he was the god of wine and grain. He was associated with the bull, the goat, the leopard, and with twining plants such as ivy and the vine.

EROS – The Roman Cupid and god of love. In one tradition, he was the son of Aphrodite, but in the Olympian creation myth of Hesiod, he appeared very early on, after Gaia.

GAIA – The original Great Mother (Mother Earth) the goddess worshipped by the Pelasgians, the prehistoric inhabitants of Greece.

HADES – The Roman Pluto, king of the underworld kingdom of the dead, also known as Hades. With his brothers Zeus and Poseidon, he formed a triad of, respectively, Sky, Sea, and Earth.

HEPHAESTOS – The Roman Vulcan, this lame god was the divine blacksmith, and husband of Aphrodite.

HERA – The Roman Juno and sister-wife of Zeus. Originally a sky goddess, her epithets of *Pais*, the 'Maiden', *Teleia*, the 'Fulfilled', and *Chera*, the 'Solitary' evoke the lunar trinity – new or waxing (maiden); full (mother); waning (crone). *Boophis*, or 'cow-eyed', Homer's epithet for her, links her with the cow.

HERACLES – The Roman Hercules. His name means 'glory to Hera', although Greek myths present Hera as his enemy. The twelve labours which she imposes on him are said to symbolize the twelve months of the solar year through which he, a solar hero, must toil in service to her, the moon goddess, thus revealing more ancient lunar–solar imagery beneath the surface narrative.

HERMES – The Roman Mercury, he was a trickster, a dream-bringer, the god of travellers, the guide of souls – *Hermes Psychopompus* – and the messenger of the gods. He also invented the lyre. He wore winged sandals, a winged helmet, and carried the caduceus, a winged staff around which two snakes entwine.

HESTIA – One of the first Olympians according to Hesiod, she was a fire divinity like Hephaestos, but of a more domestic nature, being goddess of the hearth. The Romans knew her as Vesta, whose priestesses, the Vestal Virgins, tended the sacred fire in her temple.

OURANOS – Also known as Uranus, he pre-dated the Olympians and personified the sky. With Gaia, Earth, he fathered the first race of gods, the Titans.

PAN – A god of uncertain origin, his name was said to mean 'all' and there were Pans in many localities. As the goat-legged and goat-horned phallic god, he encouraged fertility in flocks. He was later incorporated into the retinue of Dionysos. His character and appearance make him a prototype of the Christian Devil.

PERSEPHONE – The Roman Proserpina, she was, under the name Kore, the daughter of Demeter, and as Persephone, the wife of Hades.

POSEIDON - The Roman Neptune, he was god of the sea and, as the 'Earth-shaker', the bringer of earthquakes. The ram, the bull and, later, the stallion were sacred to him. He fathered the ram with the golden fleece which Jason brought back from Colchis.

RHEA – Wife of Cronos, she was probably of Cretan origin and personified the earth. As such, and as the mother of the Olympians, she came to supplant Gaia.

ZEUS – The Roman Jupiter or Jove, he was overlord of the Olympian pantheon. As the Great Father, he claimed universal paternity and procreative power. He was chiefly a sky and weather god, the thunderbolt being his weapon. The bull was sacred to him.

PICTURE CREDITS & ACKNOWLEDGEMENTS

Front cover: Poseidon (Gilles Mermet/AKG, London)
Back cover: Athene, Greek vase painting (Musée Vivenel, Compiegne/ Erich Lessing, AKG London).
Endpapers: Theseus and the Minotaur, mosaic (Erich Lessing, AKG London); p. 1 Greek vase painting of warriors, (Muzeum Narodowe/Erich Lessing, AKG London); p. 2 Medusa, mosaic (Archaeological Museum, Sousse, Tunisia/Gilles Mermet, AKG London); p. 9 Triumph of Poseidon and Amphitrite, mosaic (Musée du Louvre, Paris/ETA); p. 10 Venus de Milo (Musée du Louvre, Paris/AKG London); p. 11 Silver tetradrachma (Jan Vinchon Numismatist, Paris/ETA); p. 13 Fresco of Apollo (Museo Capitoline, Rome/WFA); p.14 Marble relief, the Three Muses by Praxiteles (Athens, National Archaeological Museum/Erich Lessing, AKG London); p.16–17 Mount Olympus (Erich Lessing, AKG London); p.18 Mother Goddess, Thebes (AAAC); p. 19 Greek sculpture, birth of Aphrodite (Museo Nazionale, Rome/Erich Lessing, AKG London); p. 20 Gorgon's head, Etruscan (Pergamon Museum, Berlin/Erich Lessing, AKG London); p. 21 Birth of Zeus, Roman sculpture (Museo Capitolino, Rome/Erich Lessing, AKG London); p. 23 Greek sculpture, Head of the Cyclops Polyphemus (Museum of Fine Arts, Boston/Erich Lessing, AKG London); p. 24 The Farnesian Hercules (National Museum of Archaeology, Naples/Erich Lessing, AKG London); p. 26 Terracotta relief of Scylla (British Museum, London/Erich Lessing, AKG London); p. 28 Greek vase painting, Birth of Athene (Musée du Louvre, Paris/Erich Lessing, AKG London); p. 30 The Parthenon (WFA); p.31 Artemis from the Parthenon Frieze (Acropolis Museum, Athens/Erich Lessing, AKG London); p. 32 Greek vase painting, Apollo and Artemis (Kunsthistorisches Museum, Vienna/Erich Lessing, AKG London); p. 35 Greek vase painting, Dionysos (Erich Lessing, AKG London); p. 37 Head of Dionysos (Musée du Louvre, Paris/ETA); p. 38 Prometheus creating Man, Roman sculpture (Musée du Louvre, Paris/Erich Lessing, AKG London); p. 40 Venus of Capua (National Museum of Archaeology, Naples/Erich Lessing, AKG London); p. 41 Jupiter (National Museum, Budapest/Erich Lessing, AKG London); p. 43 Greek vase painting, Athene (Musée Vivenel, Compiegne/Erich Lessing, AKG London); pp. 44–45 Ditz and Cameron Brown; p. 46 Minoan bull (Archaeological Museum, Heraklion/Erich Lessing, AKG London); p. 47 Dionysos, Greek vase painting (Munich/Erich Lessing, AKG London); p. 48 Apollo and Artemis, from the Temple of Apollo (Antiquario Palatino, Rome/WFA); p. 50 Piombino Apollo (Musée du Louvre, Paris/ETA); p. 51 Relief of a muse (Archaeological Museum, Istanbul/Erich Lessing, AKG London); p. 52 Gold wreath, Chalcidice (© R Sheridan/AAAC); p. 53 Syrinx Player (© R Sheridan/AAAC); p. 55 left: Gold libation bowl (© R Sheridan/AAAC); right: Gold quiver from tomb of Philip II (© R Sheridan/AAAC); p. 57 Minoan sculpture (Archaeological Museum, Heraklion/Erich Lessing, AKG London); p.59 Actaeon and Artemis, mosaic (Soueida Museum/Jean-Louis Nou, AKG London); p. 60 Death of Actaeon, Greek sculpture (Musée du Louvre, Paris/Erich Lessing, AKG London); p. 62 Gold disc with head of Athene (© R Sheridan/AAAC); p. 63 Europa and the Bull, mosaic (Landesmusuem, Oldenburg, AKG London); p. 65 Europa and the Bull, vase painting (Kunsthistorisches Museum, Vienna/Erich Lessing, AKG London); pp. 66–67 Ditz and Cameron Brown; p. 69 Orpheus, mosaic (Archaeological Museum, El Djem/Gilles Mermet, AKG London); p. 70 Orpheus killed by the Maenads, Greek vase painting (Musée du Louvre, Paris/Erich Lessing, AKG London); p. 73 Ditz and Cameron Brown; p.74 Head of Hermes, (Kunsthistorisches Museum, Vienna/Erich Lessing, AKG London); p. 76 Venus of Arles (Musée du Louvre, Paris/Erich Lessing, AKG London); p. 77 Aphrodite and Eros, Greek vase painting (Musée du Louvre, Paris/Erich Lessing, AKG London); p. 78 The Theft of Persephone (Kunsthistorisches Museum, Vienna/Erich Lessing, AKG London); p. 81 Aphrodite holding an apple (Courtesy Bruce McAlpine, London/WFA); p. 82 Juno (Museo Nazionale Roman delle Terme, Rome/Erich Lessing, AKG London); p. 83 Gold bracelet (© R Sheridan/AAAC); p. 84 Flying Eros, (Kunsthistorisches Museum, Vienna/Erich Lessing, AKG London);

p. 85 Gold diadem from Santa Eufemia (© R Sheridan/AAAC); p. 86 Greco-Roman glass vase (Musée Guimet, Paris/Erich Lessing, AKG London); pp. 88–89 Parthenon (Erich Lessing, AKG London); p. 91 Athene (National Museum of Athens/WFA); p. 92 Head of Medusa, mosaic (Archaeological Museum, El Djem/Gilles Mermet, AKG London); p. 94 Hermes (Musée du Louvre, Paris/Erich Lessing, AKG London); p. 95 Lion from Artemision, Delos (© R Sheridan, AAAC); p. 97 Heracles kills the Nemean lion, Greek vase painting (Musée du Louvre, Paris/Erich Lessing, AKG London); p. 98 Heracles fighting the Hydra, Greek vase painting (Musée du Louvre, Paris/Erich Lessing, AKG London); p. 100 The Return of Hephaestus, Greek vase painting (Kunsthistorisches Museum, Vienna/Erich Lessing, AKG London); p. 102 Gold and agate tiara (© R Sheridan, AAAC); p. 104 Atlas (National Museum of Archaeology, Naples/Erich Lessing, AKG London); p. 105 Hercules and the Apples of the Hesperides, (Museum, Olympia/Erich Lessing, AKG London); p.106 Heracles and Cerberus, vase painting (Musée du Louvre, Paris/Erich Lessing, AKG London); p. 107 Detail from gold necklace (© R Sheridan/AAAC); p. 108 The Triumph of Neptune (Archaeology Museum, Sousse, Tunisia/Erich Lessing, AKG London); p. 110 Theseus kills the Minotaur, Greek vase painting (Musée du Louvre, Paris/Erich Lessing, AKG London); p. 111 Minoan fresco, Palace of Knossos (Archaeological Museum, Heraklion/AKG London); p. 113 Icarus and Daedalus, Pasiphae and Artemis (National Museum of Archaeology, Naples/Erich Lessing, AKG London); p. 114 Theseus and Ariadne, mosaic (Kunsthistorisches Museum, Vienna/Erich Lessing, AKG London); p. 116 Part of the *Argo* (© R Sheridan, AAAC); p. 117 Ditz and Cameron Brown; p.118 Sarcophagus relief, Jason in Colchis (Kunsthistorisches Museum, Vienna/Erich Lessing, AKG London); p. 119 Minoan snake goddess (Archaeological Museum, Heraklion/Erich Lessing, AKG London); p. 121 Jason stealing the Golden Fleece (Museo Nazionale Romano, Rome/WFA); p. 122 Medea kills one of her sons, vase painting (Musée du Louvre, Paris/Erich Lessing, AKG London); p. 125 Leda and the Swan, mosaic (Archaeological Museum, El Djem/Gilles Mermet, AKG London); p.126 Minoan fresco (National Archaeological Museum, Athens/AKG London); p. 129 Gold 'Mask of Agamemnon' (National Archaeological Museum, Athens/AKG London); p. 131 Red terracotta cup, combat at Troy between Apollo, Ajax, Athena and Hector (Musée du Louvre, Paris/ETA); p. 133 left: Corinthian helmet (© R Sheridan/AAAC); right: Bronze arrow head (© R Sheridan/AAAC); p.134 Bronze figure of Ajax (Collection George Ortiz/AKG London); p. 135 Eos goddess of dawn with body of Memnon killed by Achilles (ETA); p. 137 Relief of Trojan Horse (Mykonos Museum/AKG London); p. 139 The Ship of Odysseus, (Musée du Louvre, Paris/Erich Lessing, AKG London); p. 141 Ithaca (Erich Lessing, AKG London); p. 143 Blinding of Polyphemus by Odysseus, Greek vase painting (Bibliotheque Nationale, Paris/Erich Lessing, AKG London); p. 145 Gold necklace (© R Sheridan/AAAC); p. 148 Odysseus tied to the mast by the sirens (British Museum, London/WFA); p. 151 Poseidon, bronze sculpture (Munich Museum/Erich Lessing, AKG London); p. 152 Odysseus killing the suitors, Greek vase painting (Berlin/Erich Lessing, AKG London); p. 153 Allegorical relief of 'The Apotheosis of Homer' (British Museum, London/WFA); p. 154 Dionysos and Semele, Greek vase painting (National Museum of Archaeology, Naples/Erich Lessing, AKG London).

Abbreviations

WFA – Werner Forman Archive
AAAC – The Ancient Art and Architecture Collection Ltd
ETA – E.T. Archive

Publishers Acknowledgements

The Publishers would like to thank Corinne Asghar, Claire Graham, Marie Lorimer, Alison Lee, Hilary Sagar and Juliet Standing for their invaluable help with this book.